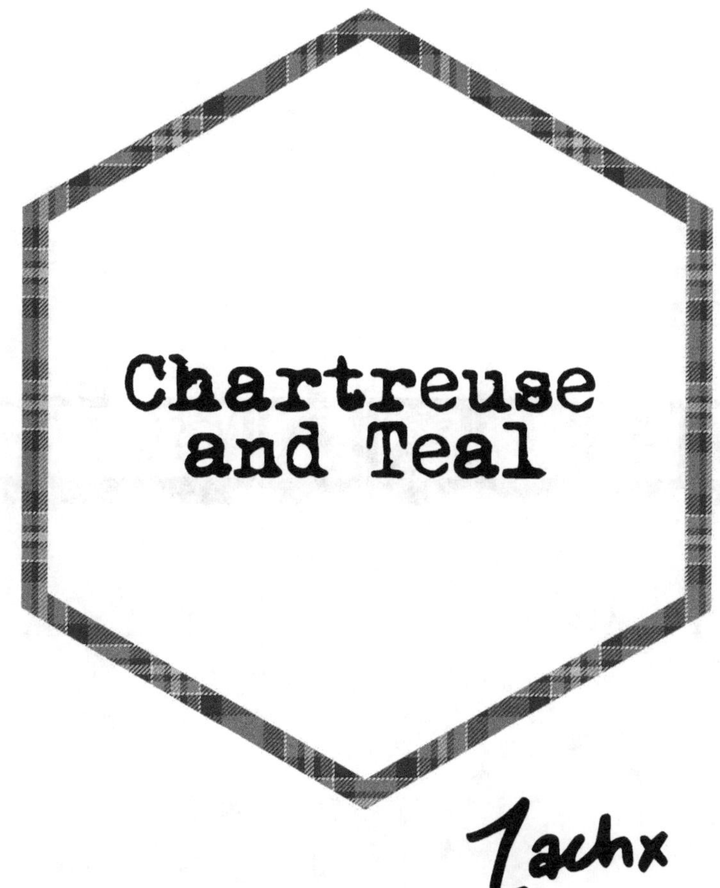

Zachx

zachx.com

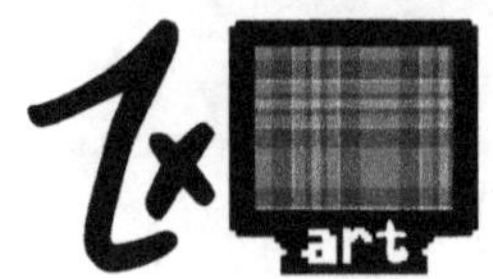

Other works by Zachx:

Articulation of the Physical, Mental, and Spiritual

Art, Illustration, and Design by
Zachx, additional design by
Trinity Dennis (Designy Life),
editing by Jenna.

ISBN: 979-8-218-69704-4

DEDICATION:

This body of work is dedicated to my wonderful wife, Julianne. I have difficulty expressing feelings of affection and love, but I intend for this to serve as the ultimate documentation of my heart to yours. Thank you for all you do for me as well as the love you bless me with. Thank you for understanding me. There is no way I could ever adequately express how much I value and appreciate you. I wish you could see yourself through the lens that I do. I thank God that He allowed our paths to cross. I cannot fathom where I would be without you. Though we are both simultaneously dark *and* colorful, I feel that *these* are our colors. They compliment each other well, which reminds me of us (and the fact that these are both of our favorite colors... It all just makes sense to me). I love how we complement each other. We are such a complex and beautiful thing. Our story may not be complete, but here is what I know for now.

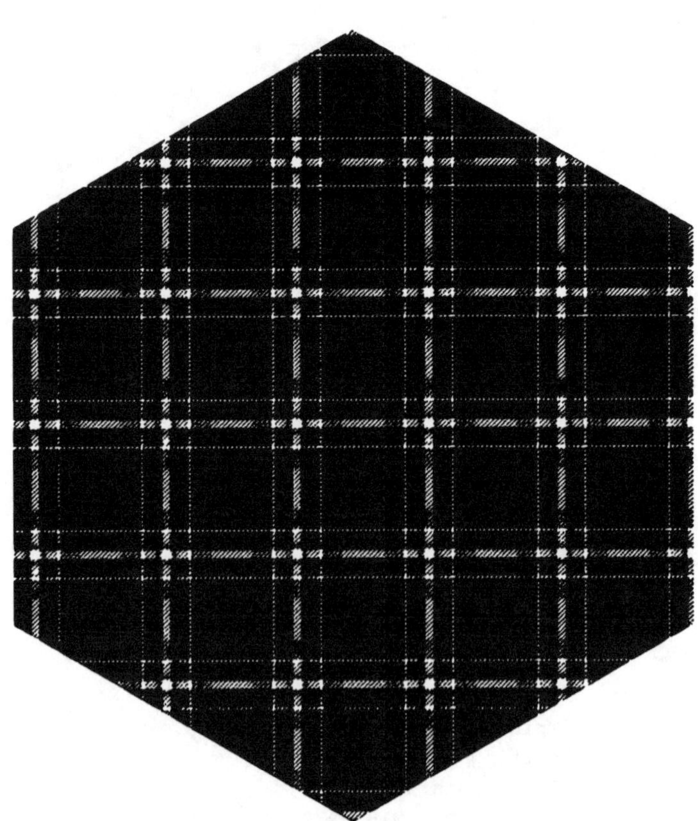

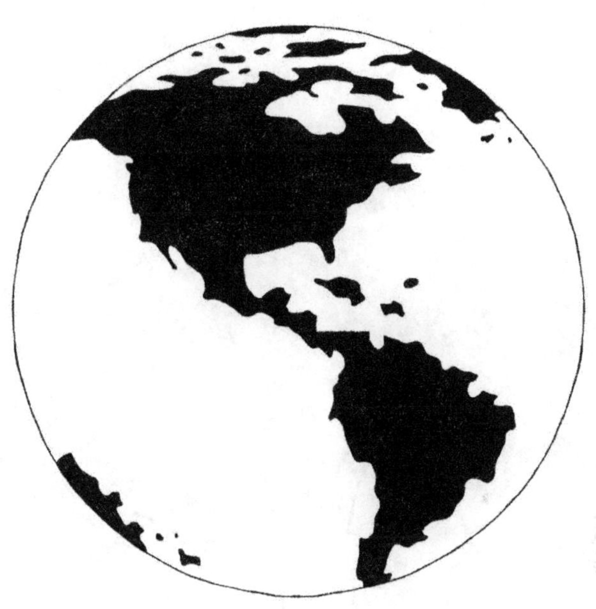

Seas and Trees (Blues and Greens) [My World]

We compliment each other as the seas do the trees.

Experiencing emotions from the blues and the greens.

When I gaze at you, my world is the reflection in my irises.

I did not plan it, but you became what my mind inhabited.

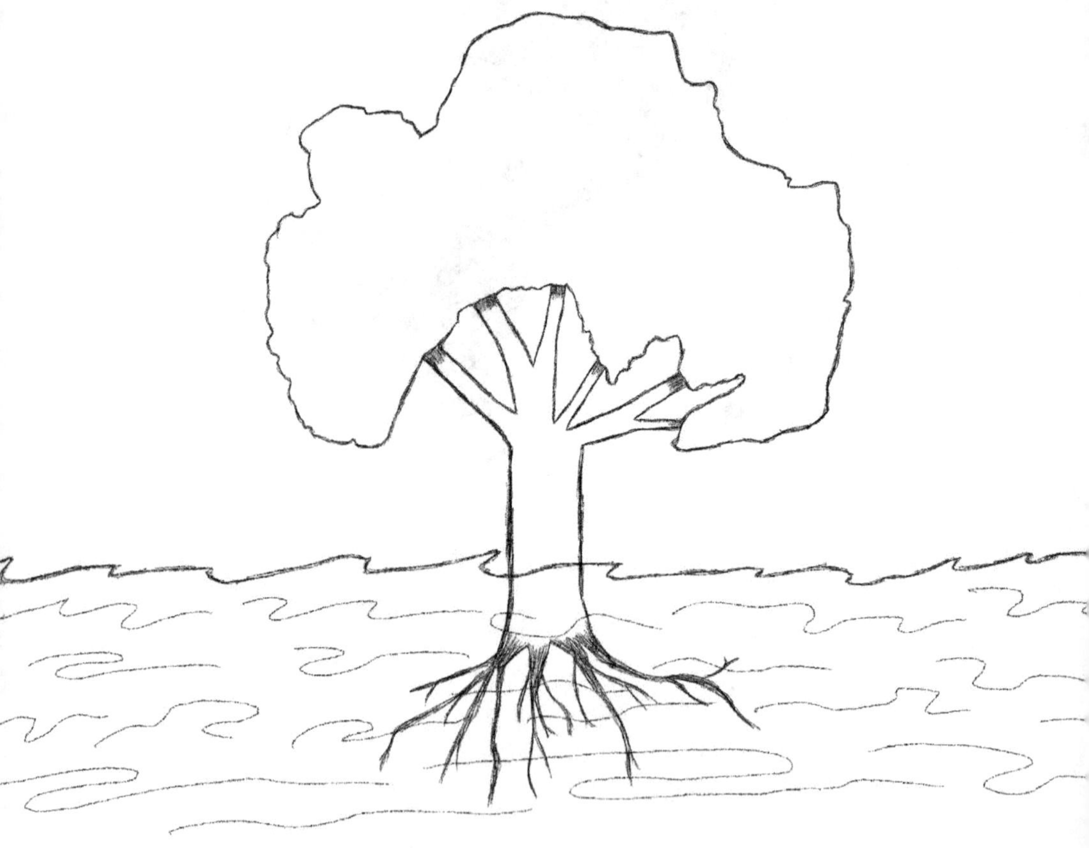

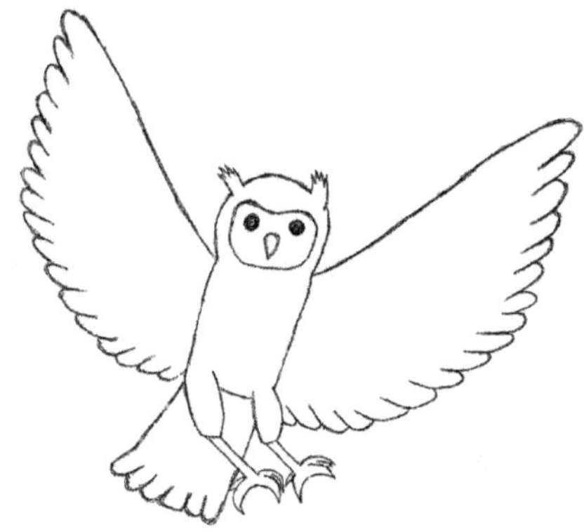

The Night Owl and the Early Bird

I am the night owl each day,

While you are the early bird.

The night air is my prey,

And you catch the worms.

I recharge in the teal dusk sky.

You witness the chartreuse sunrise.

Somehow, though we differ,

We are birds of a feather.

Vegetation

A warm congratulations to us with this.

We have a strong start on the "checklist."

Life is moving, and we are growing;

However, I cannot help but feel we are slowing.

As we plant our roots in the same soil,

We are blossoming yet fatiguing from the toil.

I cannot seem to shake the vegetative state of my emotions.

With aspirations high, weeds must not overgrow our devotion.

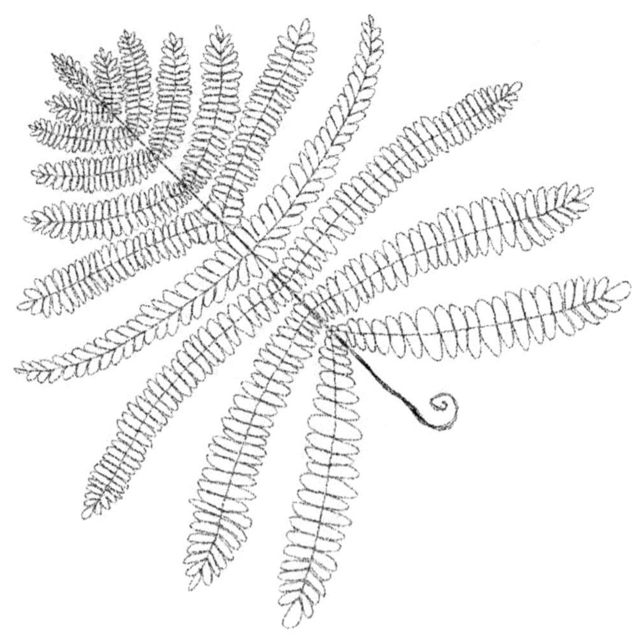

Ivy, IV

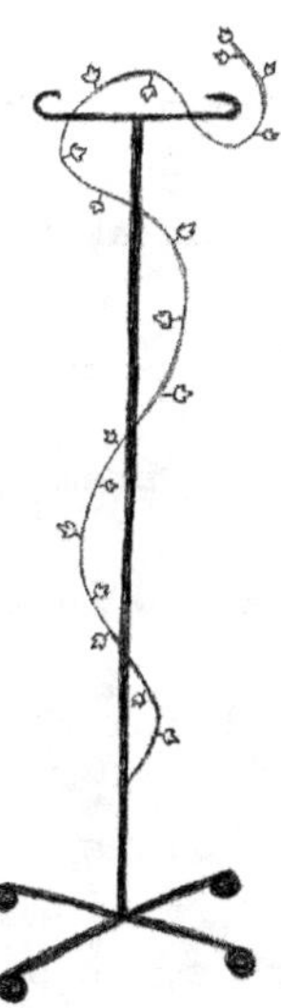

Climbing through my veins like ivy…

How I perceived love is changing;

Steadily growing and spreading—

Making its way through my body.

It is not a love that is poisonous—

An osmotic infusion, not intravenous.

Fall Risk

You have made me a fall risk.

I tried to avoid these feelings…

I thought the limbs of my heart

Were a strong enough guard

To let me remain a flight risk.

Instead, I succumbed to loving.

I do not, however, have any regrets.

You did not break my bones or my heart,

And somehow falling helped pick up my head.

You helped me break down my ramparts.

I would like to think that I have evolved;

However, I think that I have only mutated.

Regardless, it is nice to have you guide my gait

As we embrace, in sickness and health, our fate.

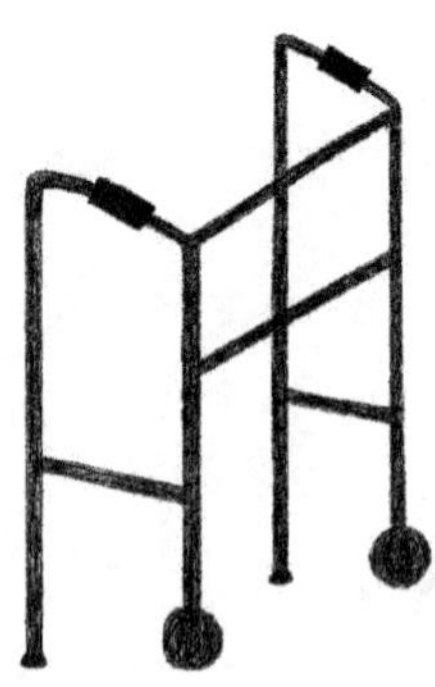

Pictures

I love the pictures of you.

When you are not around,

They make me miss you.

I like to keep them with me

To pretend that you are here.

I feel like I am losing a part of me,

But you seem to keep me sane.

You always seem to hold me together

Just like how I am holding your picture.

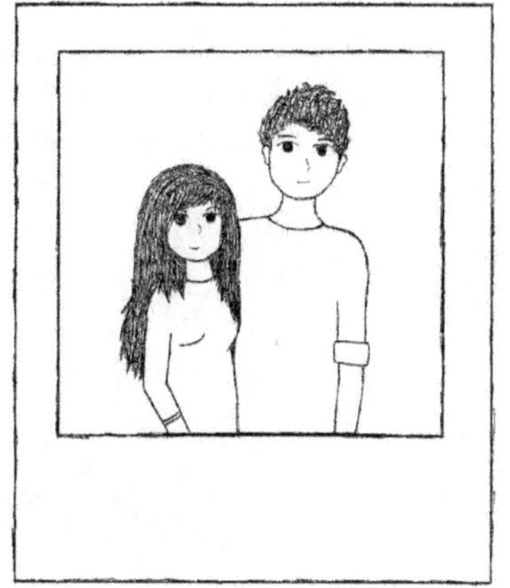

Zzz

I never thought I would desire sharing a space to sleep;

I now realize I do not have to feel alone or afraid anymore.

Sometimes, I miss you while you sleep next to me…

Somnolence has borrowed you pro tempore.

I try to seek you through my sleep walking.

I try to speak to you through my sleep talking.

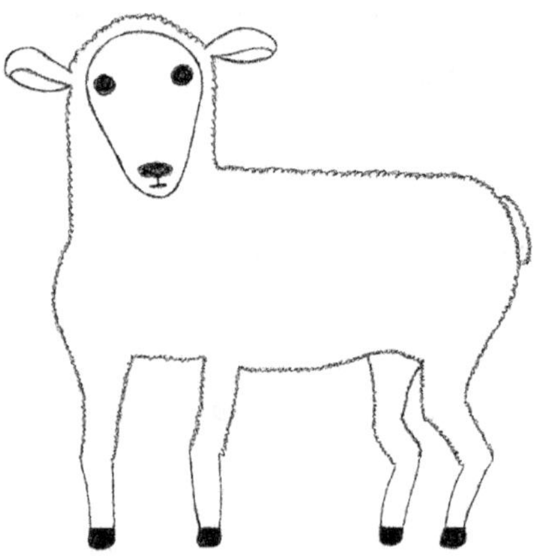

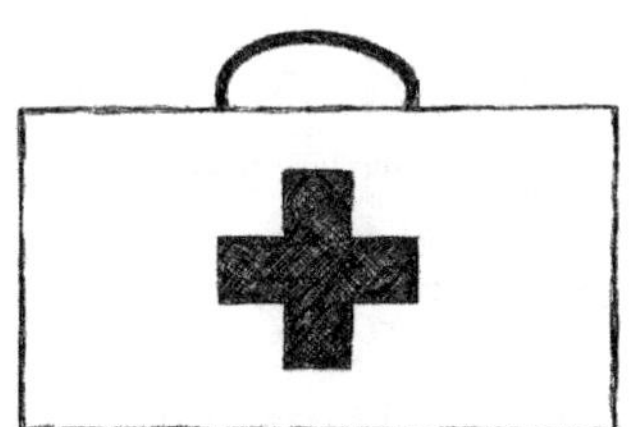

Clinic

If only I could hold your brain,

But not in such a morbid way.

To caress each fear until they fade

Into sparks of hope and patched fragments.

As I aim to keep your thoughts sane,

I often fail to adequately convey

All of my emotions as well as intentions.

I am honored to care for you every day.

Earthtones

You and I have many shades of many colors.

We have our highlights and our undertones,

But we never fabricate or sacrifice our values.

I lack in some areas—you taught me I make up for it in others.

I apologize that I cannot provide affection without prose,

But this method is documentation of my love's deep hues.

I create, embrace, and utilize all of my art, not as a crutch,

But a tool to assist my understanding of myself and us.

With this method, I can process the world around me

As well as my emotional state while regulating.

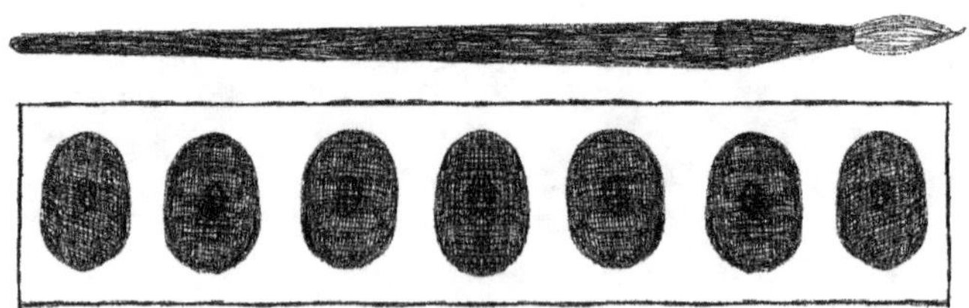

Aromatherapy

The scents that you claim

Renew my brain when you are away.

These aromas become therapy,

Unlocking sweet memories,

When they lace the air I breathe.

Even when I did not actively think,

They evoke jubilant feelings.

Though only subconsciously,

These emotions vividly overtake me.

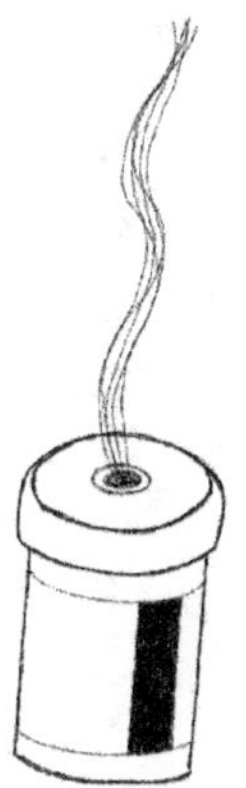

In Case of Electrical Fire

There I was on fire and filled with static electricity.

I could not muster up the kinetic energy

To alter that fixed, stationary position.

As much as I attempt, I cannot force my disposition.

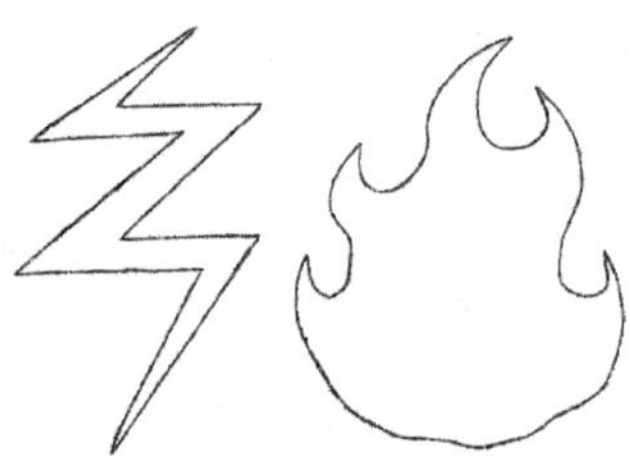

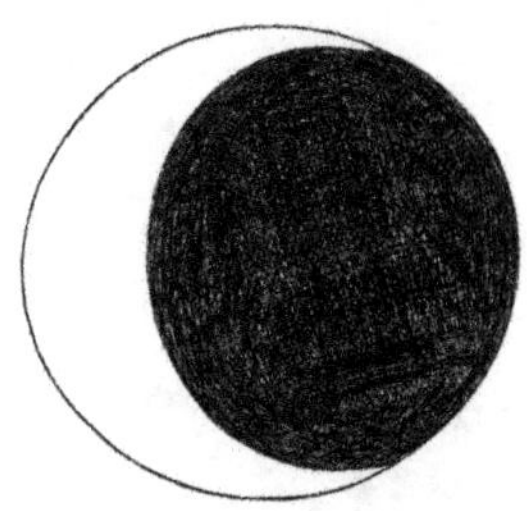

Nightshift

As your mind wanders into somnolence,

Sometimes it forgets what is beyond eyelids.

Rest easy knowing that I have the nightshift.

Often you handle the daybreak's bids,

And respond to the late nights' darkness.

Sweet dreams because I will work the nightshift.

Literature

I suppose it is my own fault for being frequently misread.

I am constantly misunderstood with a misleading cover

And opposition bookmarked between my pages.

You, however, have always grasped my existence.

Though for others, I can dictate the next thing to say, I dread

Fumbling my own social interactions and continuing to utter.

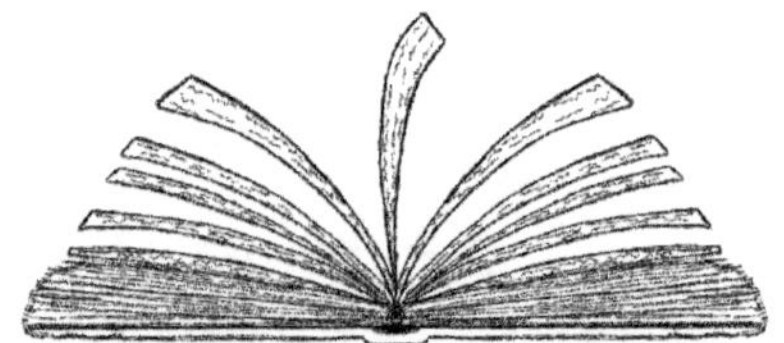

Appreciate

I appreciate you for all you do.

Every day, your value seems to increase—

It remains high—my ignorance is only decreasing.

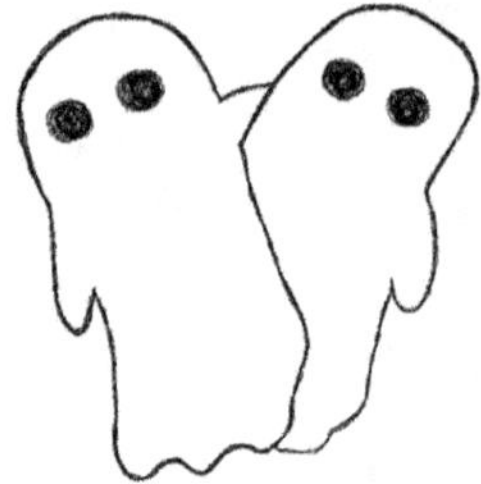

Soulmates

Does it sound insane that I want to embrace you so intensely that you pass through my flesh and bones?

That is how close I want to keep you. I desire your ghost embracing my soul.

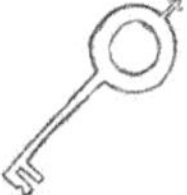

To Be Known

Nobody truly knows me like they think they do,
And that is the fault of my own.

You, however, do because I allowed you through
Those gates, and it is nice to be known.

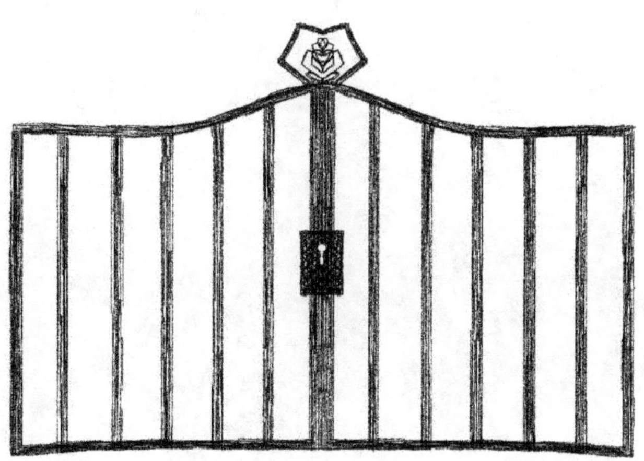

Dried Flowers

You are better with time,

Especially to an attentive eye.

Your colors deepen and are refined.

The beauty that is beheld is redefined.

You have become who you are—it is divine.

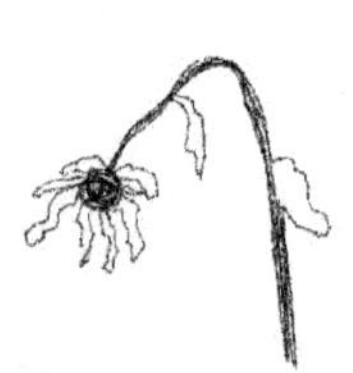

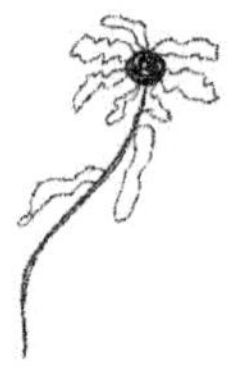

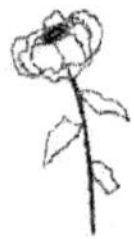

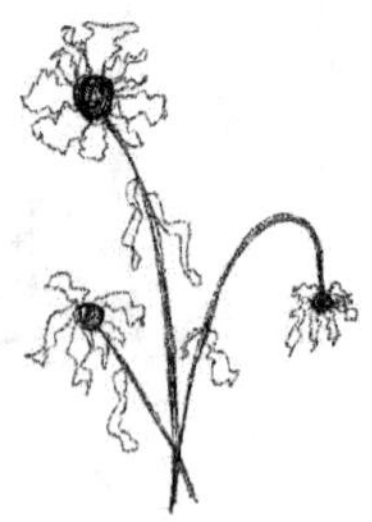

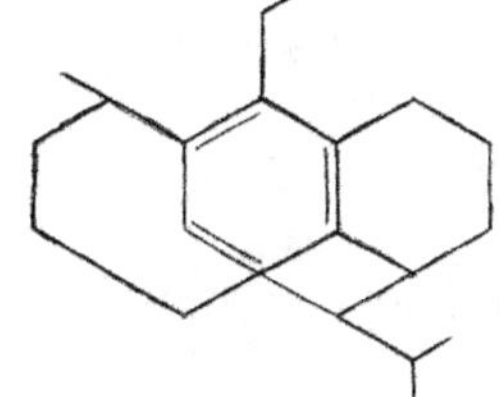

Chemistry

Somewhat polar opposites are we,

Yet we have strands in between that meet.

We exhibit strong compatibility

That at times is without obvious readability.

Florida

My temperament is like the sunshine's rays,

And yours is as the ocean's waves.

My temperature may rise with my heat,

But your logic is calming waters from the deep.

We planted ourselves where we belong.

The climate seems to mimic how we get along.

Your scattered rain is chased by my sunny days,

And my heatwaves are tamed even in a humid phase.

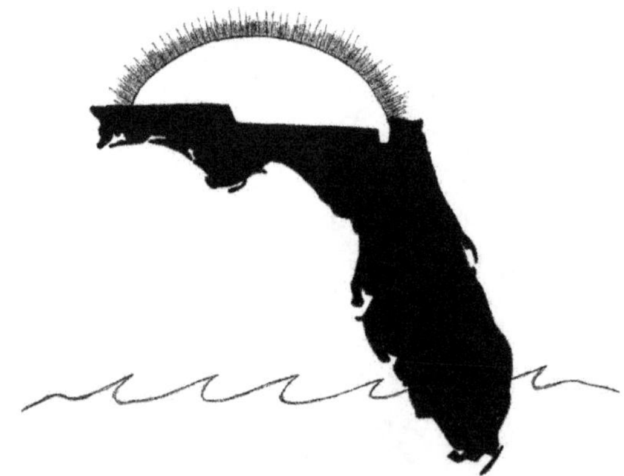

Nightride

I love those nighttime interstate rides

With the music seasoning the air

As the streetlights and moon duel to illuminate

The landscape under those deep indigo skies.

All while we sit in those bucket chairs

Profoundly feeling each moment…so intimate.

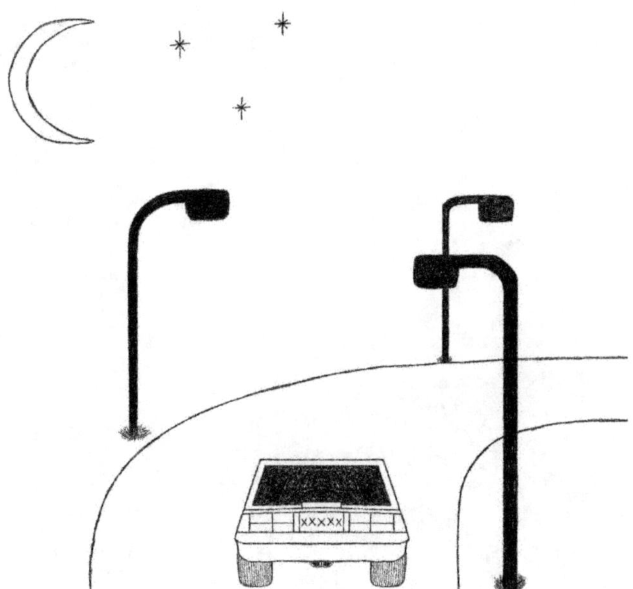

Cascades

I often reflect on when I sat in solitude in the enclosed cabin of my vehicle.

I pleaded with God aloud as tears cascaded over the ridges of my zygomatic bones.

He met my plea and forged a path to make the continuation of our story possible.

Now we adventure to seek life's wonders and waterfalls wherever we go.

Light Pollution

We can pretend the light pollution is the twinkle of the stars and the shimmer of the moon

Because with you, memories of visiting the most desolate places become an extravagant scene.

We compliment each other—comparing and contrasting—turning sparkles into gleams.

As we face the darkness in this life, we can polish what the world pollutes.

The Hero and the Sidekick

Neither of us fully embody the hero or the sidekick.

We both adapt and fill the part as it requires it.

The main character and the supporting role.

I love our power to adapt and achieve our goals.

The two of us have different skills and abilities,

But we negotiate this life together while conquering.

We are a power couple—with you, I am superhuman.

We may not don masks or capes, but always have a plan.

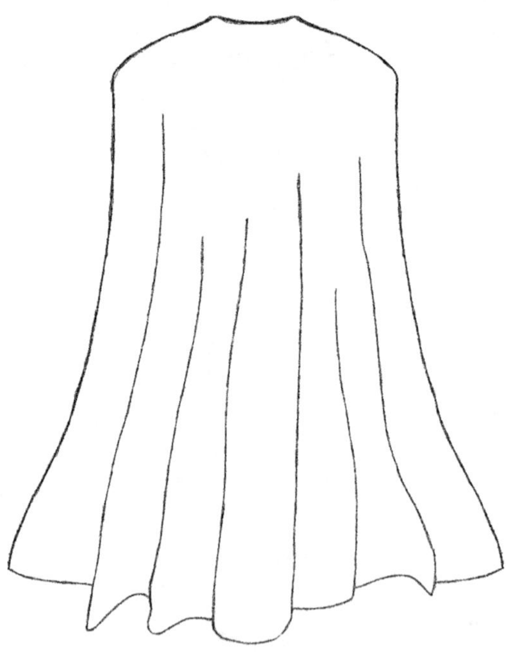

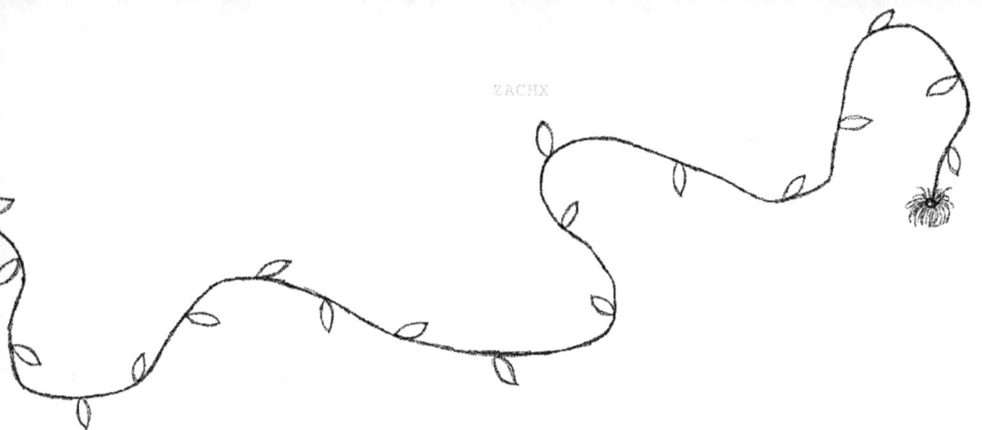

Growing Older

It would be untrue if I claimed that growing older did not cause fearfulness in my mind.

It is a contradicting feeling because I would love to backtrack, but you would not be there.

The past is a small garden hosting fresh greenery with small buds, and here we are now lush and thriving.

I still fear growing older, but it is more bearable with a helpmeet like you in my field.

After all, you did help the flora of my being to mature, bear fruit, and become resilient in time.

Nostalgia and youth will always tug at my heart, but with you, my remaining days, I want to share.

Though, at times, depression may be at the gate, we can help each other reclaim the land victoriously.

Alone, we may not be sufficient, but together we can carry all of the tools that we need to wield.

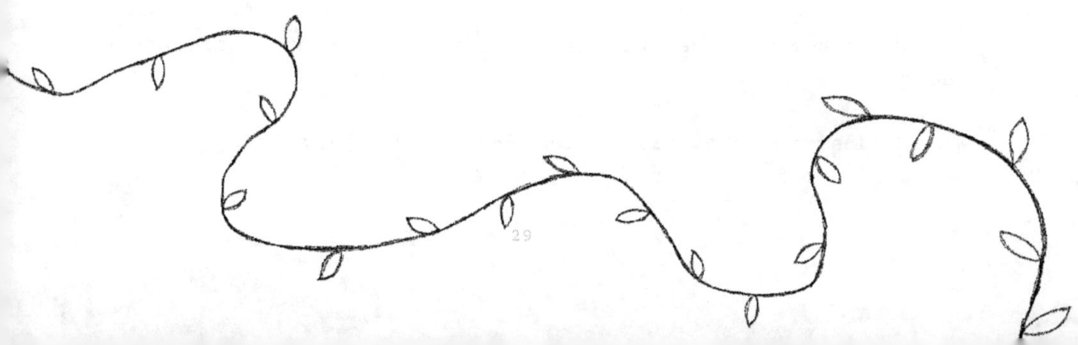

Therapist

I know that many years of trauma have stained your brain,

And your emotions, chained by exposed wires, latch onto your heart to conduct your conduct.

Any wrong move or false start seems to electrocute your body and send you into shock.

Your nerves conduct electricity throughout your system that elicits static,

And I volunteer to be your therapist to redirect that negative energy into your muscles to elicit strength.

I will attempt to guide you and rehabilitate those emotions that are lame.

Together, we can reduce the inflammation in your heart and reconstruct.

To prevent these negative feelings, through love, I will act as a nerve block.

With these protective and healing measures in place, we can be dynamic;

We can both heal each other as we synchronize into the same wavelength.

I will show your flesh what love is without leaving behind scars or pain.

I promise to help you feel as if you have never been struck.

All of the potential that was hidden away, I will aid you as it unlocks.

We can work towards a cure from the tragic without the means of magic.

With endearment that originates from a pure place, may it never become necrotic or faint.

Puzzles

We somehow fill each other's gaps and complete each other.

Not total opposites, but many of my strengths are your weaknesses.

Conversely, many of my weaknesses are your strengths.

Separately, our misshapen pieces do not have as many purposes to serve,

But together, they display our completed picture and bring balance.

With you, I have nothing to lose and everything to gain.

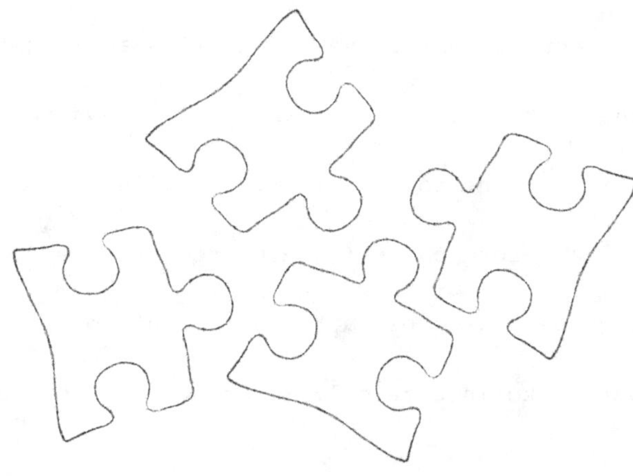

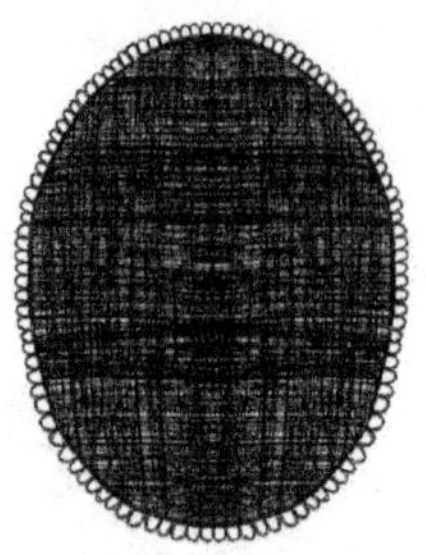

Opaque Opal

Your exterior hides the wonders of your personality.

So many animated thoughts and emotions that are not obvious—

Learning you has been a beautiful and fulfilling journey.

You shy away from displaying the array of vibrancy you possess,

But I encourage you to emerge from that shell that shields the light.

You do not have to submerge yourself in fear and doubt.

You truly are a wonder that is so bright with so much fight.

From all of the darkness, be brave and bold enough to dismount.

Remember that it is fine to be a little fragile at times

As long as you care for yourself and protect your spirit.

I will be alongside you to extract any remnants of grime.

We can etch our marks into this life through the scuffs and the polish.

Arrows and Daggers

Between your arrows and my daggers,

We can fight and defend against our enemies.

As we react very differently to situations,

While neither is sinless or completely justified,

Our unique styles are complementary as they stagger.

With each other's assistance, we can be freed

From whatever compilation of complications.

Whether long-range or close combat, we will be fine.

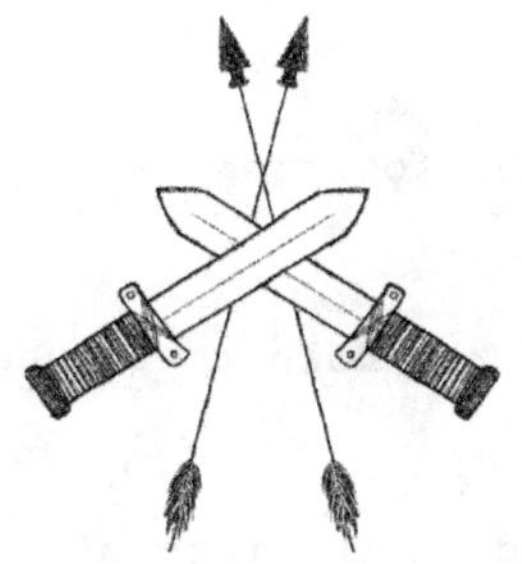

Sparks

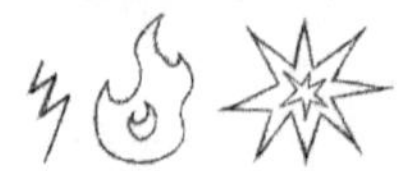

Facing each other across the aisle during transit,

In your eyes, I saw a spark that I believed was only my imagination.

We were both spoken for in that era, but while we were lost in that moment,

Nothing seemed to matter except that stirring in our spirits.

Though the sparks were there, never did we break any commitments.

While remaining friends, and at any moment, we could have commenced ignition.

I supposed it was the right person and wrong time, but now it seems senseless.

The electricity we shared was undeniable, so why did we delay it?

The sparks were in the circuits, but we kept them silent.

As things progressed in your life, the fear began to set in.

I tried to keep things ethical, so I remained a closed circuit

Until I realized that I was on fire and I could not continue in suppression.

Now with distress at the forefront of my mind, all I could feel was depression.

I had to readdress and rekindle these sparks from the dark to create illumination,

So with a match in hand in the form of a rose, I created an explosion.

A fire that burned so brightly and so unapologetically became our relationship.

From sparks, to flames, to an intricate electrical grid—we made it through devotion.

Mutts

We are just a couple of mutts

Navigating these picket-fenced yards

With no accurate category.

Something I have grown to love

Was formerly something so hard.

We embrace our unique story,

But nobody else truly wants

Us because we are just mutts.

They only want fragments of us

Because the mixture is harder to grasp and love.

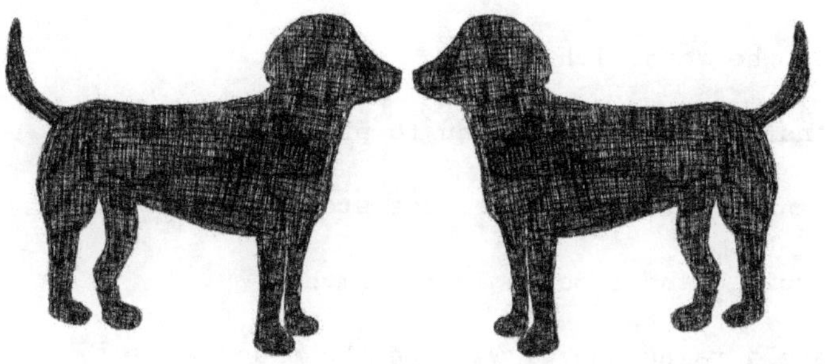

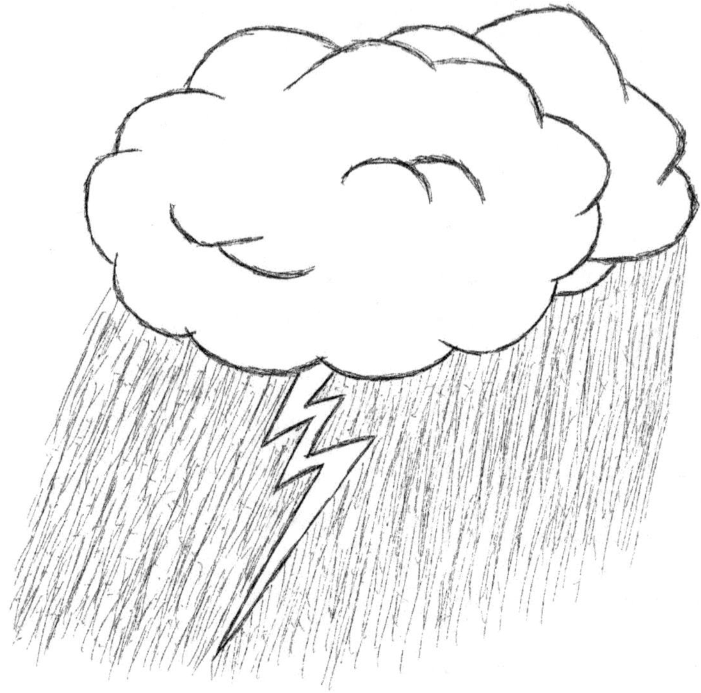

Storm

Your sorrow accumulates like the clouds

With each teardrop falling and watering the ground.

As they convert into raindrops from evaporation,

My rage, like lightning, strikes the skies

And fills the void with light,

Thus transforming each emotion to prevent stagnation.

Our combination creates a perfect storm.

Hot and cold blend into cool or warmth.

If you are a raincloud, I will be the thunder

And the lightning; I will be your protector.

Amber Embers

I do not feel adequate enough as I stand.

I apologize that I am not as strong as I would like to think I am.

I know you insist that I am the man you desire,

But it is hard for me to process those feelings through this fire.

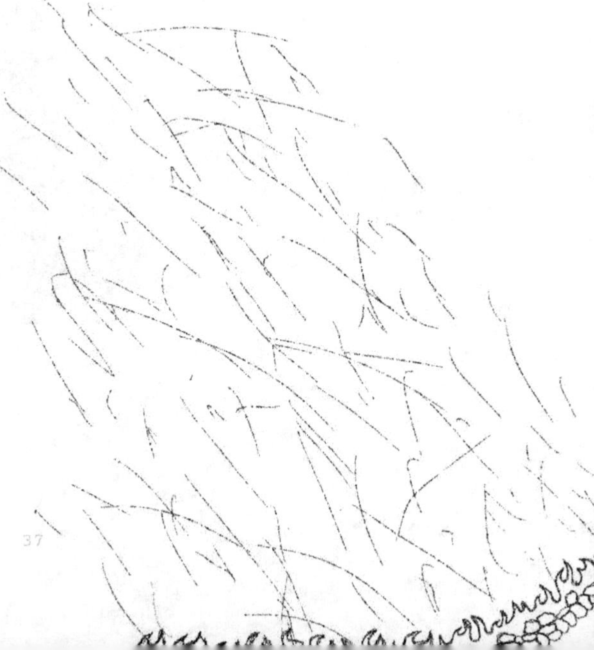

Evergreen

If only I knew how to keep my emotions evergreen.

The truth is that I love you, but sometimes I cannot access it.

It is so ironic to me that somebody like me has a bride

When emotions such as love are hard for me to abide by.

Please do not ever forget this even with the night's sheath.

My love still lives beneath the cover and will have resurgence.

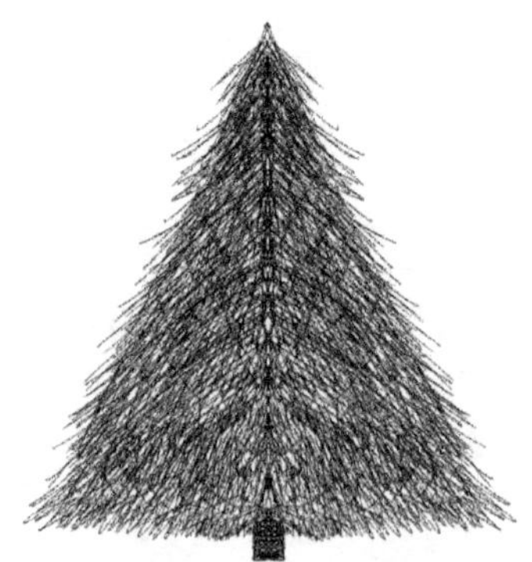

Water Table

I never meant to pour my frustrations onto you.

It was not my intent to spill my flash floods over your dew.

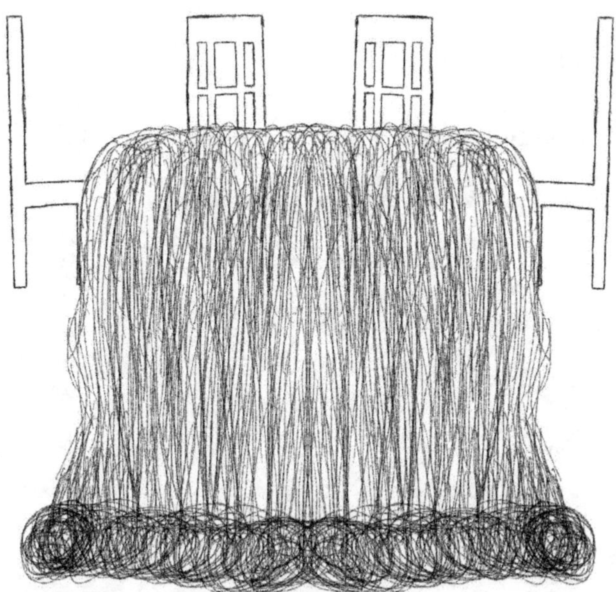

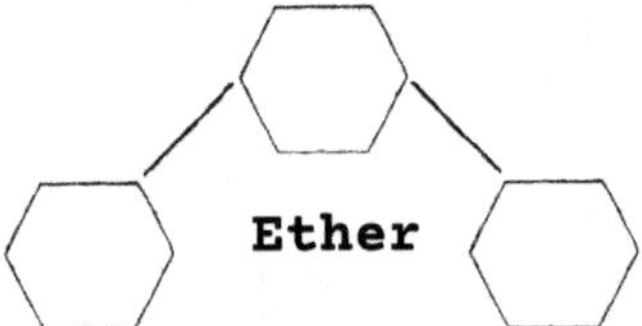

Ether

I strive to make your pain numb and dull,

But I know that I am flammable.

I am learning to let my emotions be fluid

Rather than rigid and ruined.

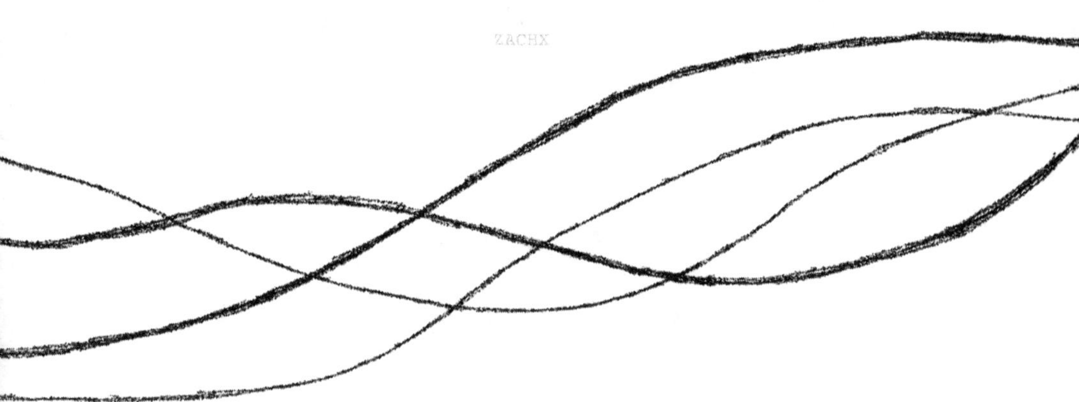

Tubes and Wires

As we navigate this life through the tubes and wires,

You can teach me how to go with the flow

While I teach you how to be more sporadic.

Restricted by the walls of society, yet within our power,

We wade the currents whether fast or slow.

Static is in our nerves and veins that we convert to dynamics.

All the cords that tangle us in life, we redirect through fires.

We will locate and clear any obstruction in any hose.

We will continue to learn life's circulation and circuits

As we go through these phases, cycles, and motions.

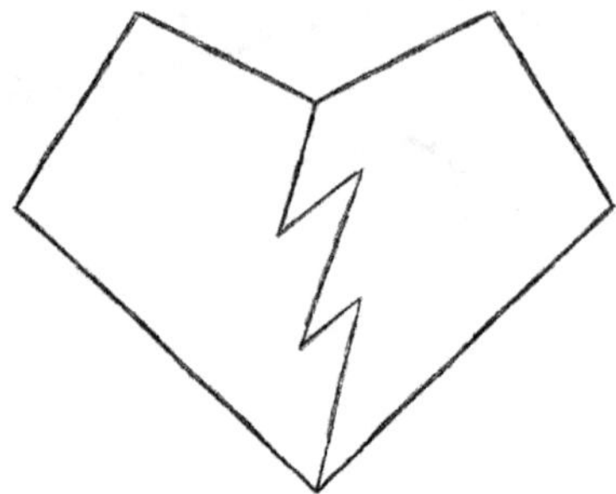

Lo Siento

Though we both often make mistakes,

I too often tend to assign the blame.

You see me in him, but that relationship has lesions.

I promise I will try to be my best version.

I have a habit of reacting before fully pondering.

That does not equate to thinking you are squandering.

I apologize in advance as well as for the history.

I will strive to avoid conflict and promote inquiry.

Currents

When our currents meet,

They play off each other.

My sporadic electricity

And your calm waters

Charge each other with attraction.

We are electromagnetic.

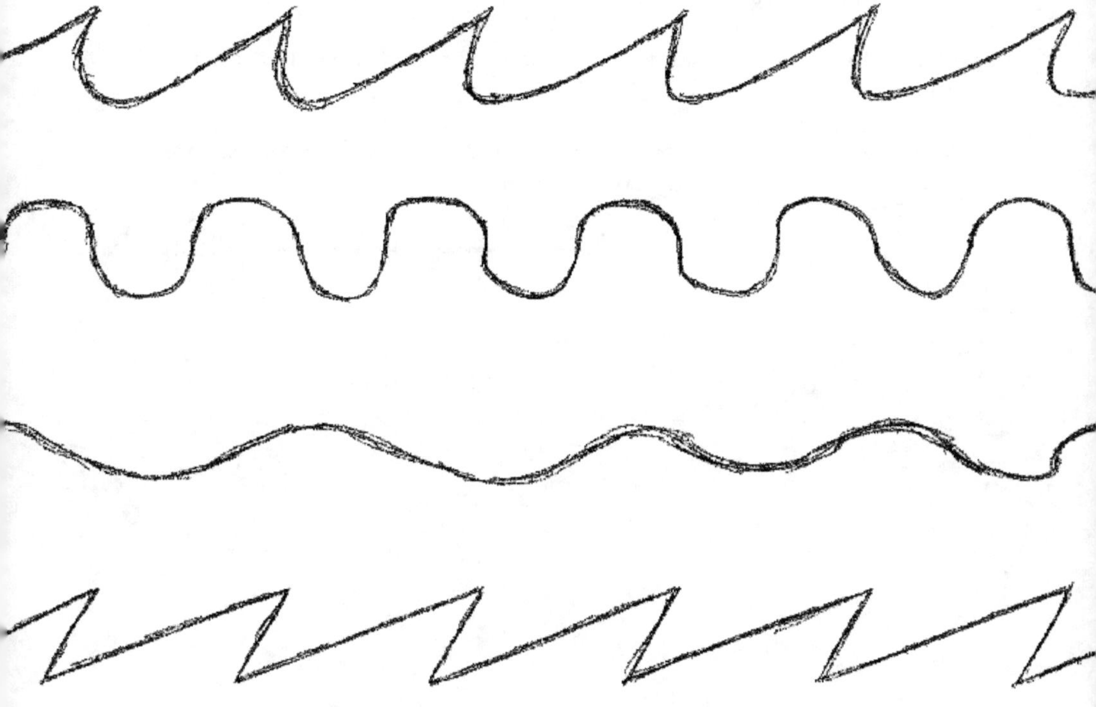

Gym to Gem

You are always there to help me exercise my fears.

Take me to the gym so I can work out my insecurities.

Show me that my anxiety is only a lie ricocheting in my mind.

I have been stagnant, but you have turned my gears.

The weight is shedding off my shoulders now that I am no longer waiting.

Now I am stronger in every way, and I intend to continue making good use of my time.

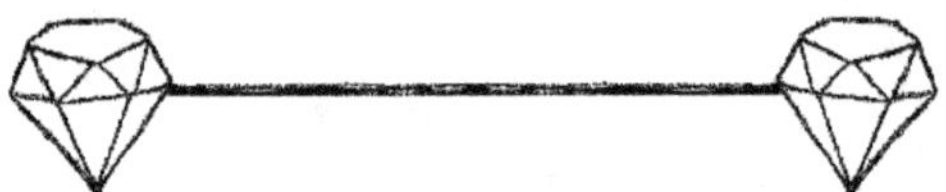

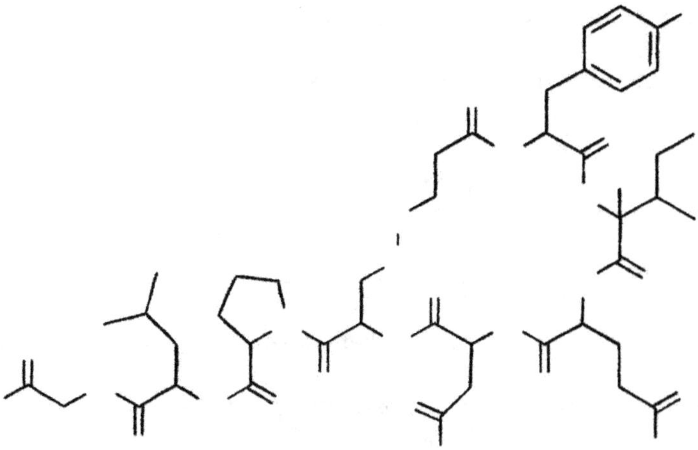

Oxytocin

As this stranger walks by,

Her essence catches my eye.

As my brain begins to recognize,

It is actually you, I realize.

The one who prepares meals,

And to my heart who heals—

It is you, where my love is sealed.

Within me, you spark such zeal.

The Class Clown and the Teacher

You became the teacher

While I remained the class clown.

I still feel like a child or a creature,

And you are good all-around.

Frequently, you teach me lessons

With your tact, grace, and class.

Education is a vacation when we are in session.

I profess my love through humorous acts.

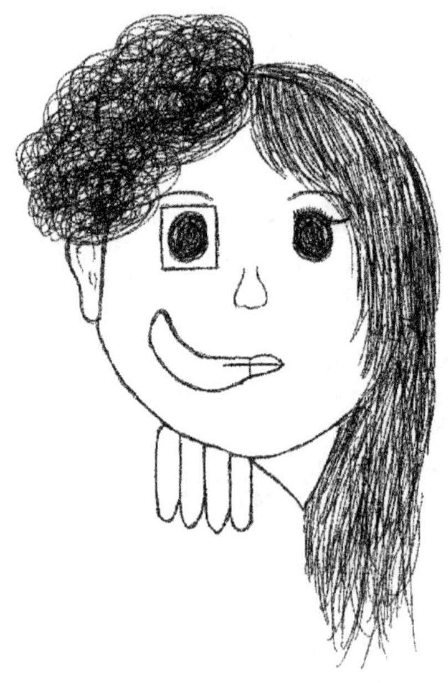

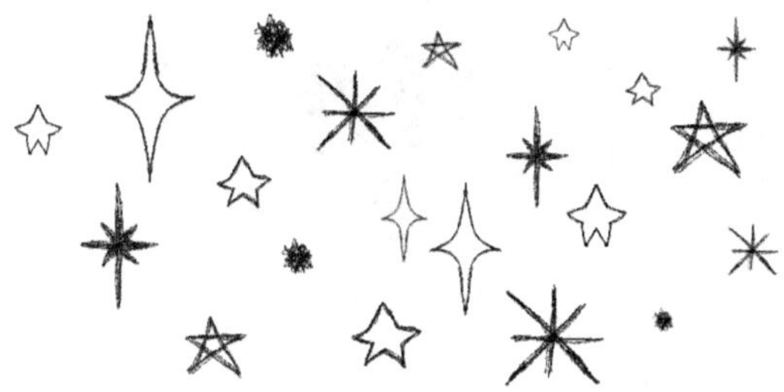

Stellar

Did God allow the stars to align

In order to make you mine?

It was not determined by Aries or Aquarius,

Nor was it a matter of rearranging constellations.

Our energy illuminates any juncture

Because a love like ours is stellar.

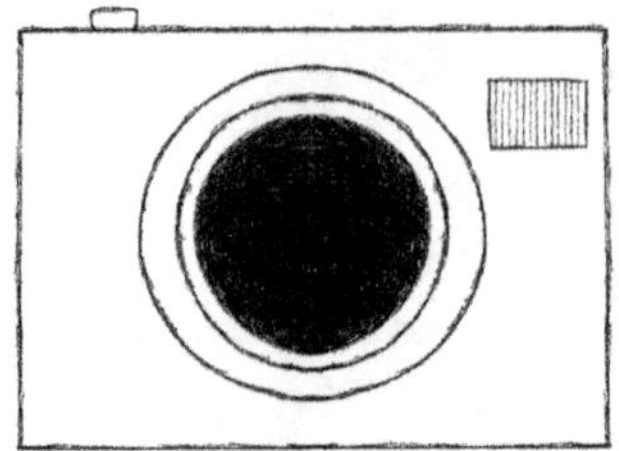

Camera

Your lens can decipher my filters,

And mine can see you, even if blurred.

If only pictures and videos

Could capture our highs and lows

In beautiful details so we can reflect

Just in case our memory is wrecked.

We refract the light inside of the darkness

To utilize each spectrum to our benefit.

I want to save each moment of us

To reminisce on all of our love.

I crave to feel every color in our album,

And I want to taste every sound as well.

I desire to hear every touch of your skin,

As well as to smell each emotion.

Also, to see every flavor of you and me.

If only a camera could record such things.

Campsite

You are the ocean and the sky,

And I am the land meeting the tide.

The rivers extend as the veins of the sea

Hydrating the Earth beneath our feet.

We sit fireside by the creek's waters

As the night becomes the author.

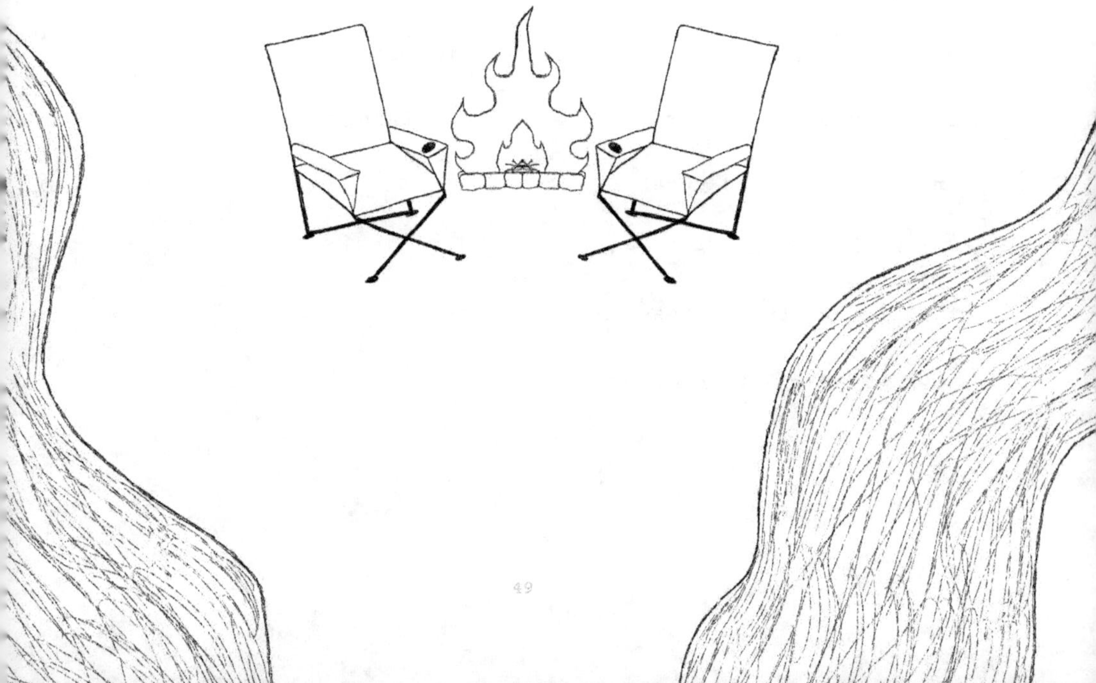

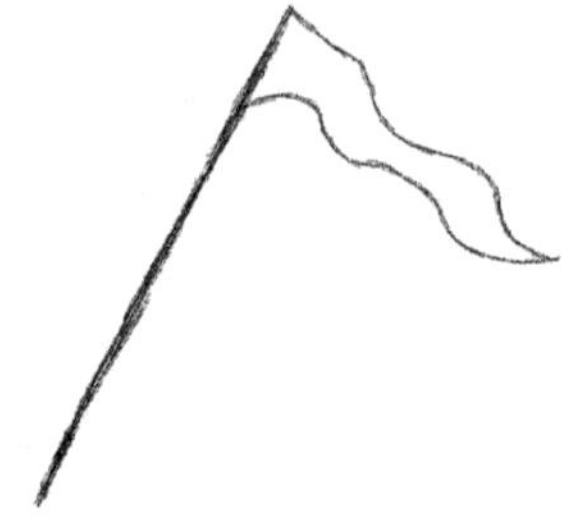

I Am Sorry When I Am Sorry

My intention is never to hurt you,

I just get so numb sometimes.

Something about the pain I cause

Forces my mind back into reality.

When my connection to love occludes,

I choose a method so unwise

That injures your heart and violates our clause.

Reflection on these errors enables my learning.

I knew you would be upset,

And I knew I would feel regret,

Yet I still uttered those things I said.

It now replays inside my head.

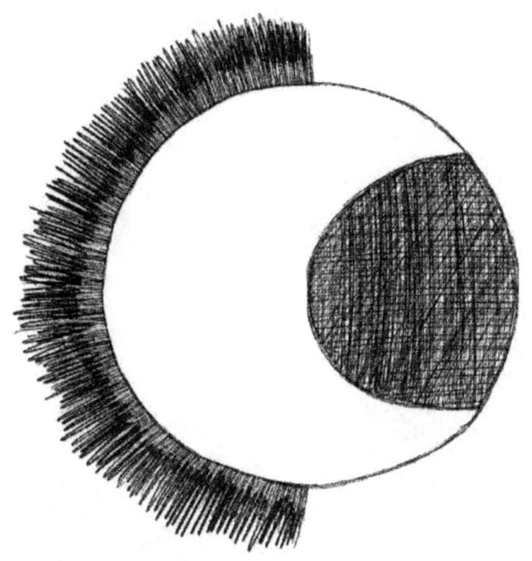

Nychthemeron

You glow in the daylight,

And I show like a night light.

Dawn is when you begin to thrive,

Meanwhile, at dusk, I am coming alive.

The daytime is the peak of your day,

And the nighttime is when I radiate.

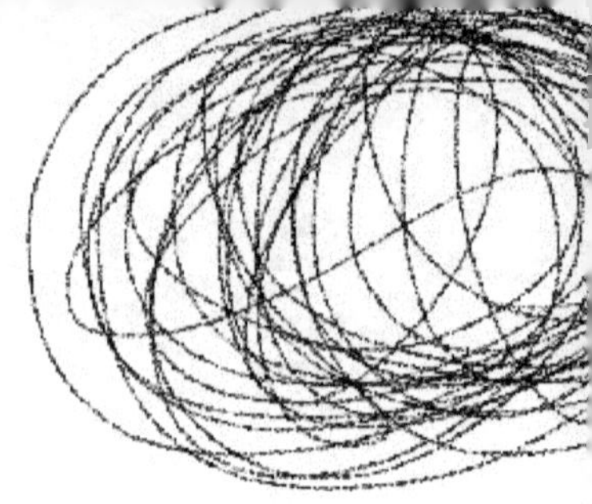

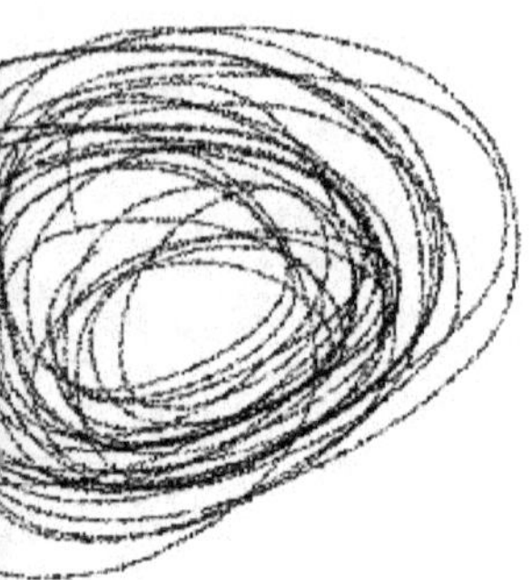

Anxieties

We share the burdens of the same curse,

But we wield the artifacts differently.

Together, for better and for worse,

We can support each other as a team.

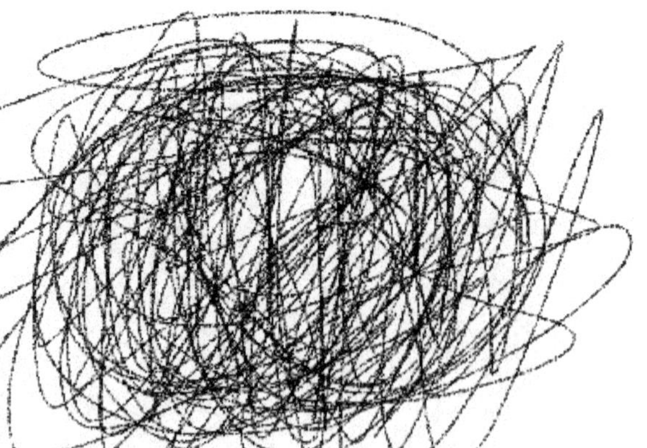

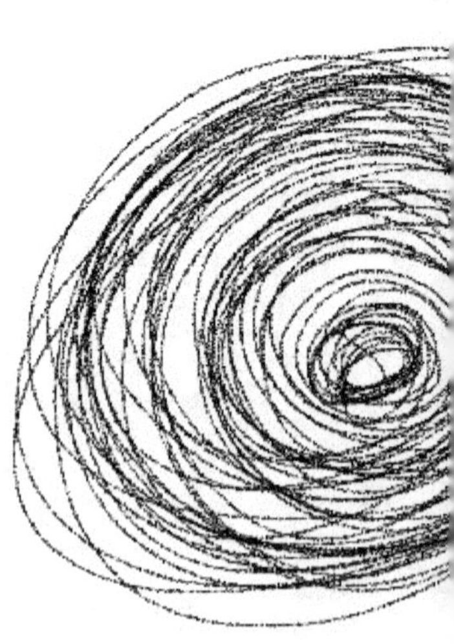

Weekends in Alabama

So we can escape for a short stay,

But not too near nor too far.

Exploring more than an average day——

Beyond the boundaries we keep at home.

To rejuvenate our spirits and heal dismay,

Yet keeping our ties at arm's length.

The wonders that lie in these landscapes

Are waiting for us to experience them.

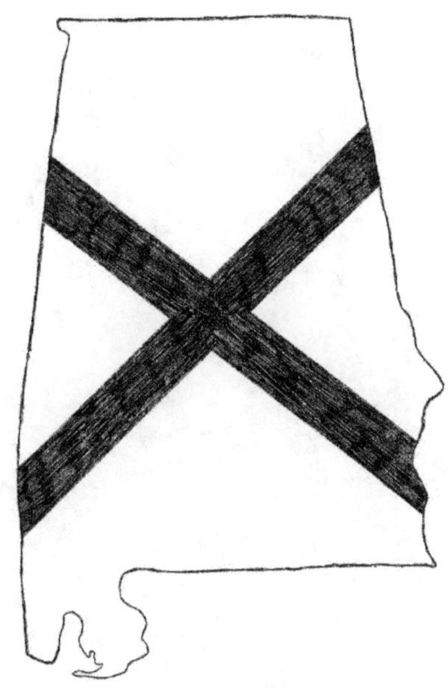

Anime

From reality, for a little while, let us escape

And experience emotions from other lives.

They may be fictional and not actuality,

But despite this, we can feel an array

Of feelings and view the ways we align.

We then can see worlds without traveling.

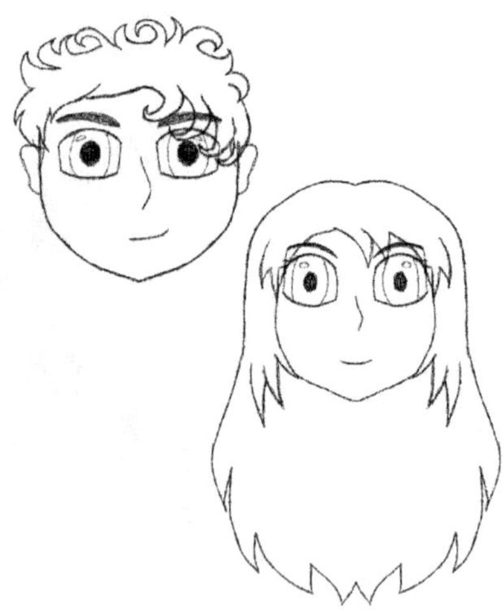

Te Amo, Mi Amor

I will utter every ounce of my love

Through the language in my blood.

I will then speak it in my native tongue

From all my soul, burning like many suns.

Color Codes

Our colors compliment each other,

Thus creating a pattern or design

That otherwise would be more bland.

We are a tapestry that is displayed

With great pride and immense joy.

We are a handsewn quilt of plaid

With every fiber dyed a particular color.

Every detail of us was paired by the Divine.

We are painted to be complementary, and

Even when we do not coordinate, we play

Off of each other's hues like iridescent toys.

We are programmed to be a match.

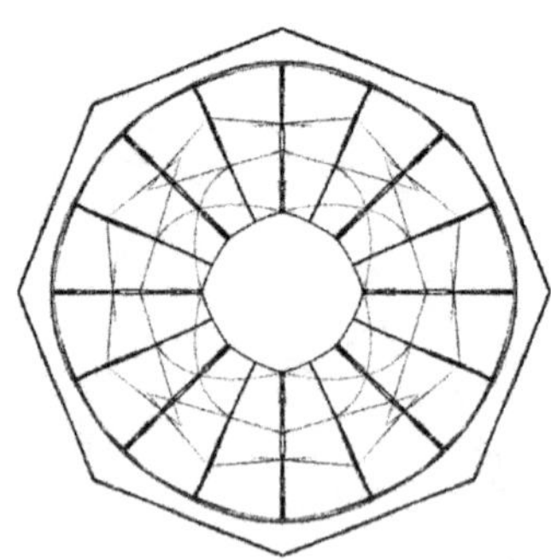

Irises

Light illuminates the Earth in my eyes—

Your irises become lanterns in daylight.

That is something I did not realize

Was a wonder I needed to visualize.

When your irises bloom in the sunlight,

I just wish I could plant them so I

Can see that beautiful sight any time.

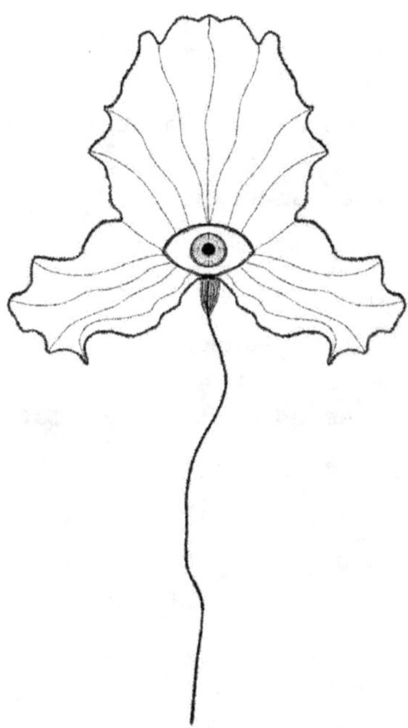

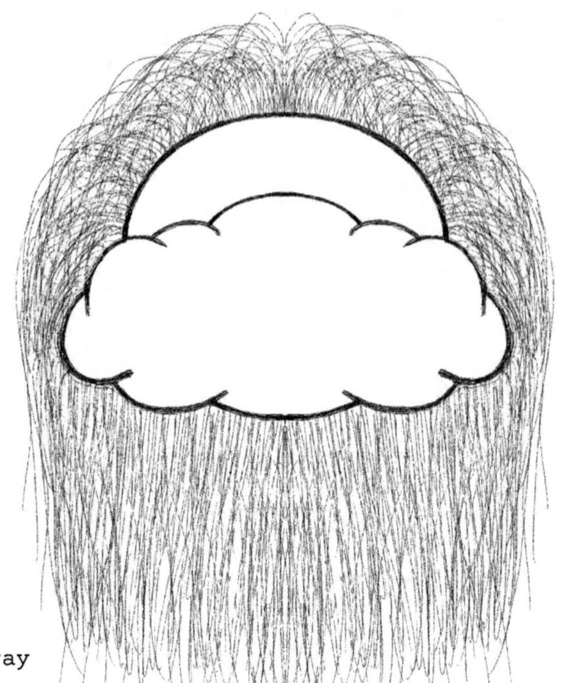

Rainshine

You remind me that the gray

That is delivered by the rain

Also deepens the hues and saturates.

It may cloud my mind, but it hydrates the land.

As the water glazes the landscape,

I realize that it allows dull things to radiate

And anything soiled to be washed away.

The drops on my skin remind me to appreciate it like the plants.

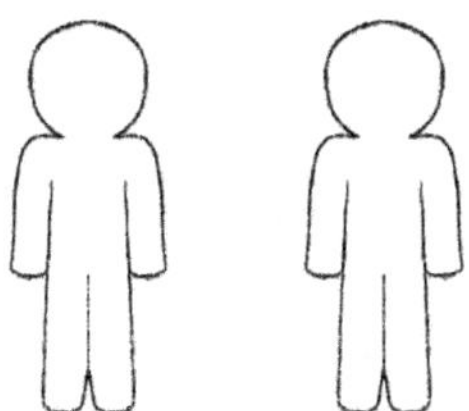

Friends to Lovers

We cannot be friends

Because we are meant

To be something deeper.

We once were in suspense,

But now have been cleansed

Into something sweeter.

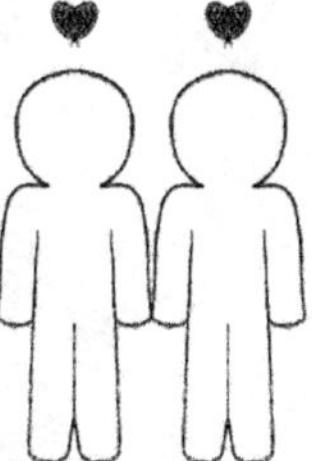

You Are a Force

Every day you amaze me.

No matter what you do,

You will always make it work.

You are a force.

You truly are amazing,

And I proudly claim you.

You find ways to open doors.

You are a force.

You have great tenacity

With passions you pursue.

You are a legend of folklore.

You are a force.

You make up where I am lacking.

You have a lens for truth.

It is you whom I adore.

You are a force.

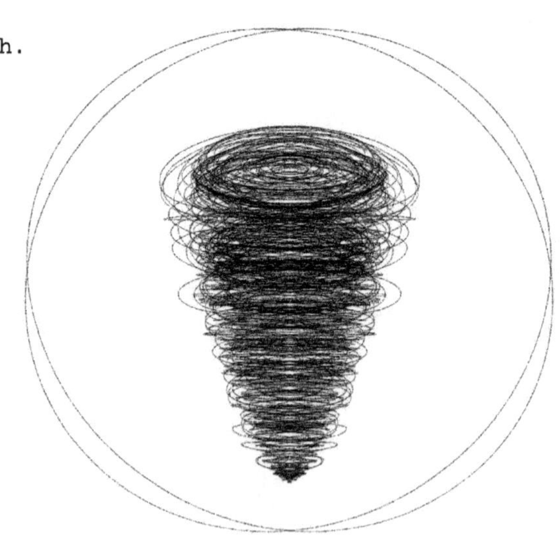

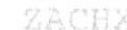

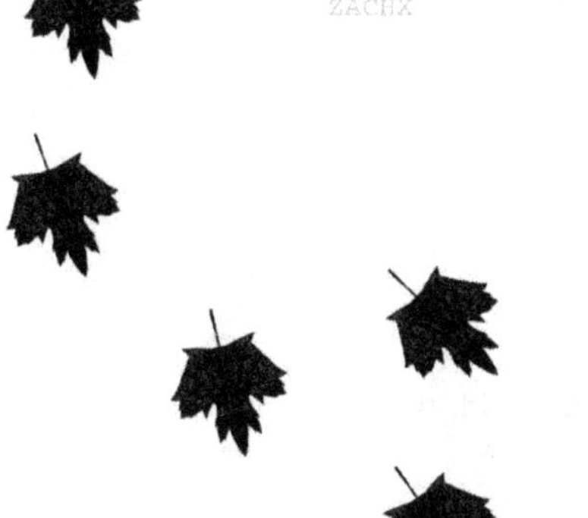

Fall

If you begin to fall behind, I will fall back.

I vow to never fall away, but only fall for you.

In the fall as the leaves change and fall, I will not.

As autumn lets the cold fall, I will keep you warm.

If the fall of man is what led me to you—to us...

Then I would fall for those tricks as well.

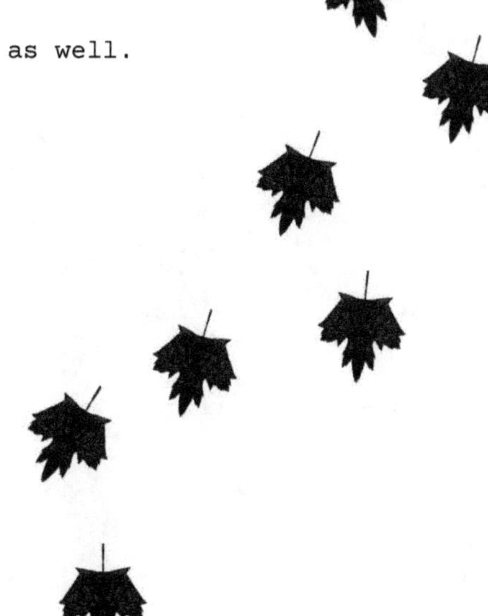

Perennial

Our love is everlasting and blooming each year.

Though we have dormancy phases, we still grow.

As our roots grow deeper, and we become established,

Together, we have absolutely nothing to fear.

We were once just buds, but now full-blown

Because we keep each other pruned and enriched.

After every frost, we flower with colors brighter

And richer than what was displayed in the previous season.

We are not planted here to die, so we keep watered

Though we may not always understand the reasons.

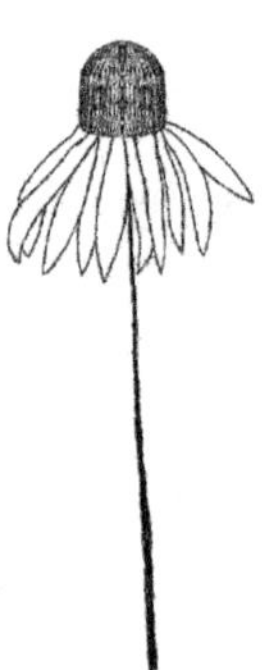

Endangered Species

We are an endangered species.

While many put themselves in a cage

In front of the world on display,

It is all a rushed facade and incompatibility.

Our love, however, is purebred,

And is not based in lust,

But fortified in absolute love

That will never be found dead.

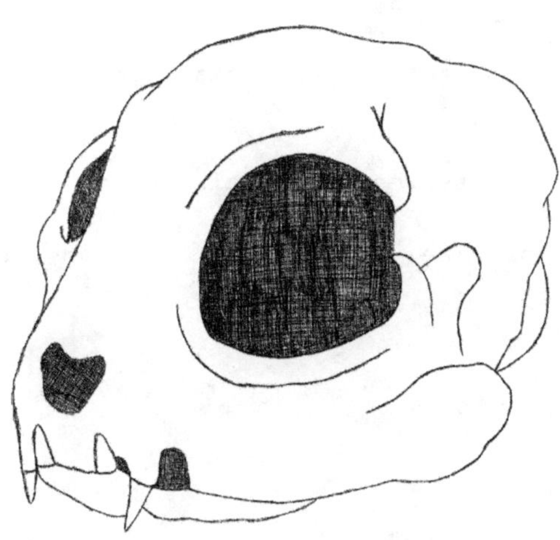

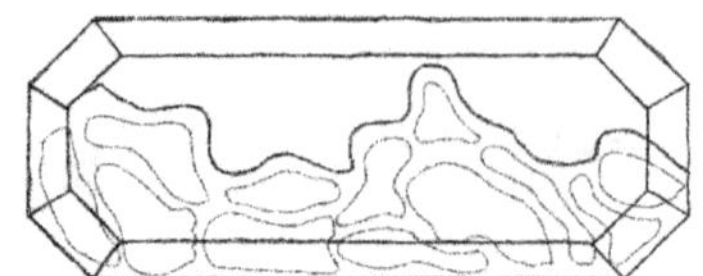

Emerald Coast

Just as the emerald waters meet the deep blue,

That is precisely how I want to exist with you.

As the healing tides renew the sands our footprints are comprised of,

I pray for rehabilitation like that over any blemish on our love.

Because of you, I wade through uncertain currents in peace

Much like the seabirds float along with the misty breeze.

The waves direct our motions just like all the perils of life,

So we harness what control we can to make the best of those riptides.

Through the seagrass, seaweeds, and all the fish in the sea,

Along the salty shoreline, and through anything, we will keep swimming.

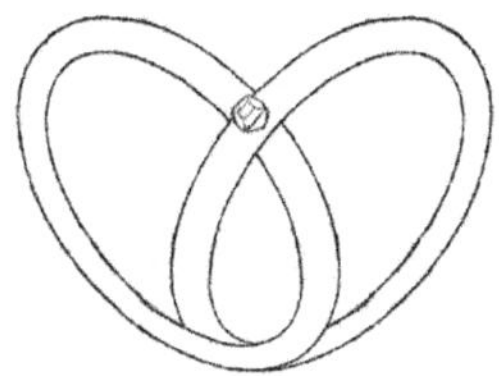

Alloy Ally

As we meld together

We are better than ever.

I was fine on my own accord,

But with you, I am reinforced.

We always can forge our frame,

And shield from the rust and rain.

Thank you because I do not deserve

To hone myself on your shoulders.

You remind me when to spare the rod

Whenever my emotions are wrought

With all my unrighteous anger.

When necessary, you are my anchor.

In my wrinkled brain, you begin ironing

To press emotions that have been stealing.

Bluegrass

In the meadow we were raised in,

We plucked the fields we played in.

Then we sang melodies together there,

Planting notes in the empty air.

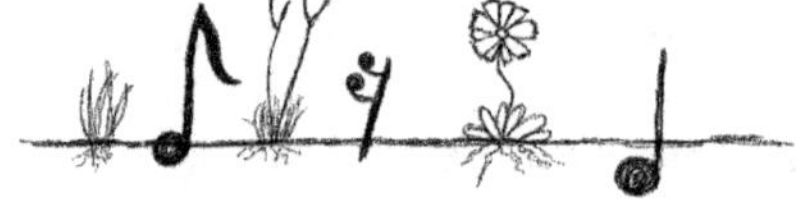

Blackwater

These emotions flow through me like water,

But it is difficult for me to wade through that river.

I keep them a secret, not because of shame,

But because they are deeply personal waves.

I know this does not translate as anticipated,

But I know that without you, I would be devastated.

I may conceal these feelings beneath brackish currents,

But that does not make my love any less valid.

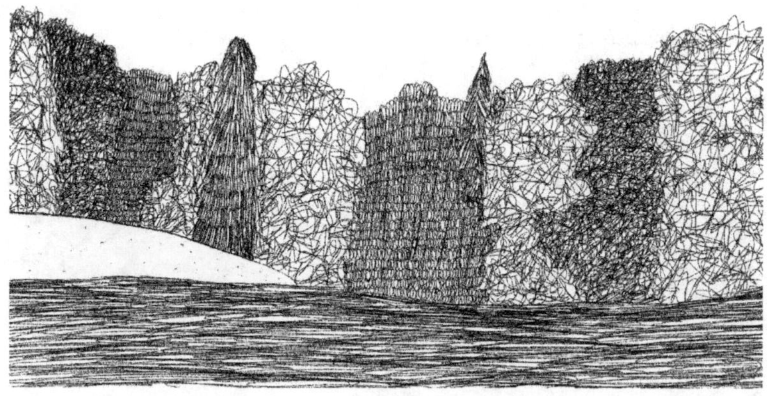

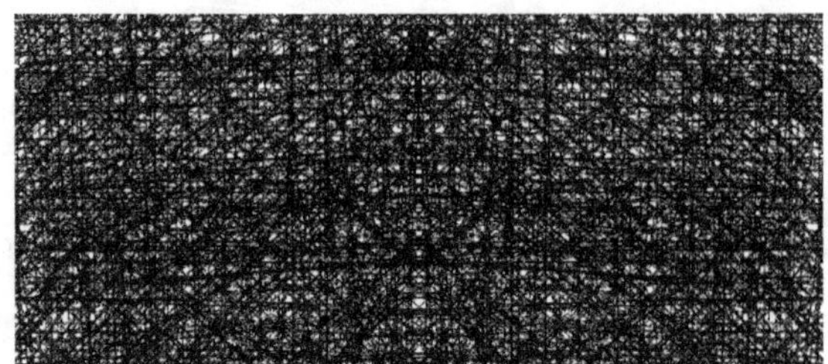

Darkness

When the blinds draped over my eyes,

A noir chariot abducted my vulnerable mind.

Peace and slumber were thieved, and I

Am only left disturbed and sleep-deprived

Because in the dead of the night,

Instead of sleeping, you had died.

Now I know how I would feel if I survived,

Though I never wanted to witness such a sight.

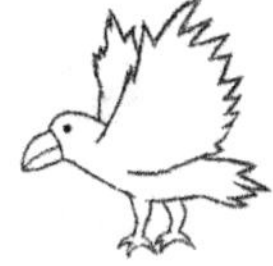

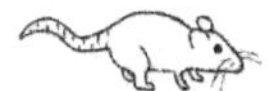

The Rat and the Raven

I feel misunderstood while you seem respected.

I feel like I am viewed as a disgusting pest,

But you are viewed as a mysterious guest.

I know that is a dramatization within my head

How your wings carry you while disease I spread.

Those thoughts, I cannot help but tread,

While I assume all the things people have said.

Buds

I wish we could be brand new and exciting again.

Those butterflies eventually forget how to fly.

New relationships are like Christmas morning as a child.

I miss that feeling, but nobody else could replace you.

I crave returning to when we were green and still friends.

Everything we did was an unspoken, exciting, new high.

I want to remain this comfortable, but with thoughts still wild.

Maybe your being away will remind these emotions how to bloom.

Please do not misinterpret these words because

You are the only flower that could give me that buzz.

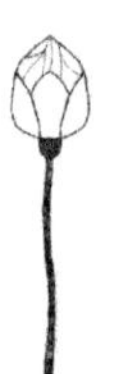
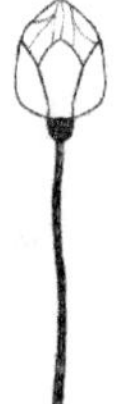

Alone (yet) with You

I feel lonely while you are away.

How have I never noticed this before?

I would not typically ask you to stay

So you could enjoy your family more,

But I think this time that has changed.

I have always been comfortable being alone,

Then you came along and taught me

That specifically with you, I can remain in my zone.

Now when you are gone, I feel incomplete.

I want you to enjoy your time, but please hurry home.

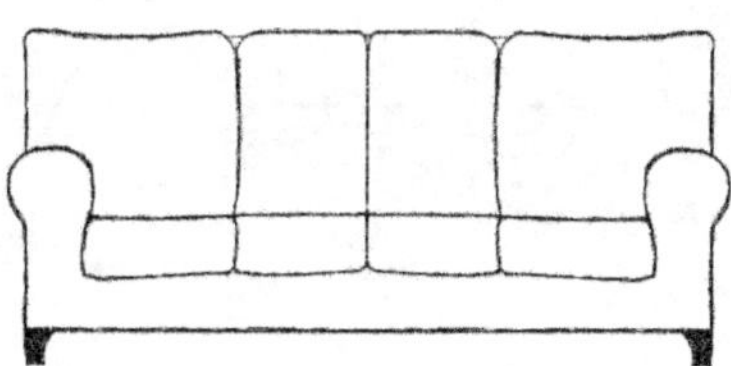

Golden Flowers, Golden Hour

Your hair and your eyes radiate in the sunlight

Just like golden flowers during golden hour.

When they are not shimmering, they are as rich as soil and flare

With blooms of sparkles in your eyes and twirls in your hair.

You may have not been made into gold, but you are golden.

At least in my eyes, and to you, I am beholden.

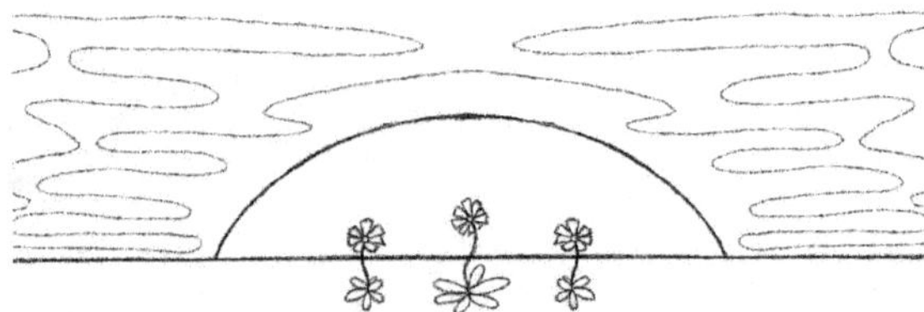

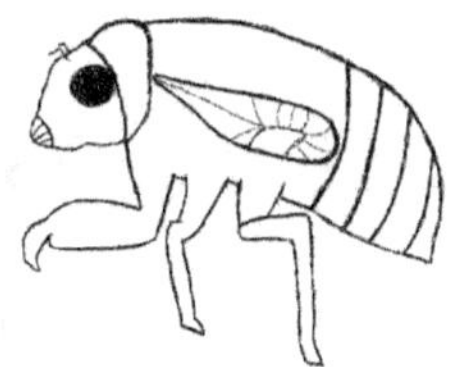

Two Nymphs

We have grown and molted, yet we are still nymphs.

We are students of this life, but we can teach what we know.

Our wings have not fully developed, but maybe will in Heaven.

As we tread the ground, we learn skills to help us reap and sow.

We spent so long underground and from the world, hidden,

But now we are shedding anxieties and starting to float.

While we emerge, we are gaining new perspectives

And healing each other while we remain equally yoked.

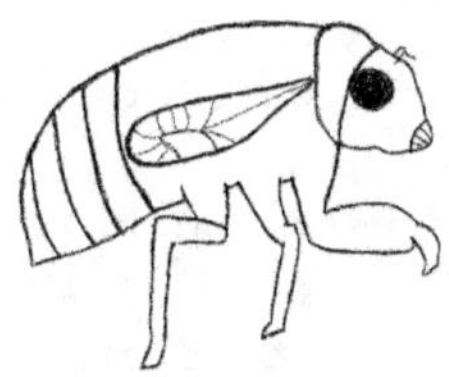

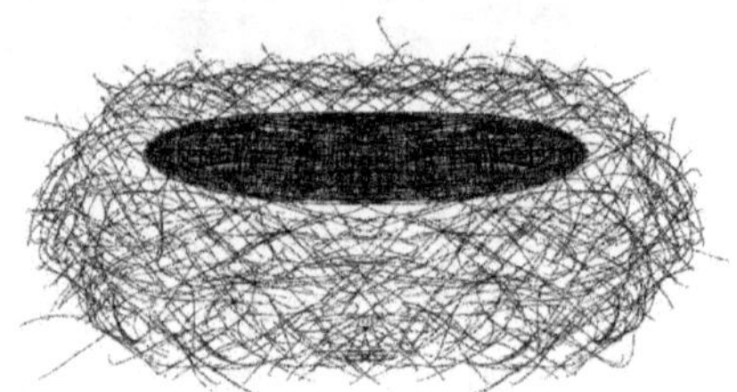

The American Robin's Nest

I know that we share the same mentality.

We want to experience life's offerings,

But we are undecided and uncertain,

Especially with something so permanent.

To be honest, that desire has never been

In my heart, but I cannot bear to prevent

You from living a life you might crave.

I fret for regrets that may linger to the grave.

I am sure, yet unsure of what I am wanting,

But these emotions continue to haunt me.

You would make a magnificent mother,

But I fear I would be a failed father.

Our nest is enough, but if our wings extend,

We can figure out how to endure the wind.

If the soil is barren and the eggs are blue,

We will create a way to harvest the fruit.

Whether there are rough waters or stormy weather,

Like birds, we will burrow, run, swim, fly, and persist together.

Berries

Why do we work so hard to produce this fruit

Just for the animals to carry it away and eat it through?

Our labors grow berries from many vines and branches.

We invest in many plants, and our sweat brings sweetness.

Success burgeons in pieces, but not the whole tree.

While we pay with burdens, it seems others gain for free.

Flowers hint that our efforts are about to flourish,

But we can only enjoy our prosperity for but a moment

Before life grazes and plucks each off the bush.

We can only delight the calm for so long before we are pushed.

As our goals ripen, it feels pleasant but also scary,

And soon after, in newly sprouted troubles, we are buried.

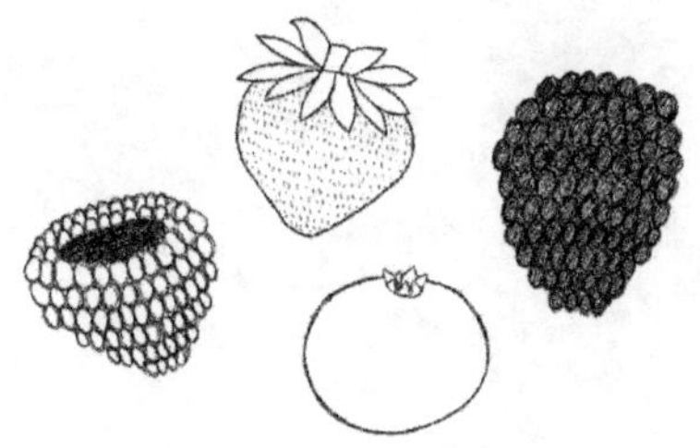

Daisies and Violets

I sit and imagine us in a field of flowers.

What a wondrous sight to behold.

Diamond daisies and amethyst violets

Saturate the mirrors of my optic orbs.

You still occupy the forefront of the hour

Even while surrounded by a beautiful glow.

How can something so gorgeous be so delicate?

I vow to be your protector against any force.

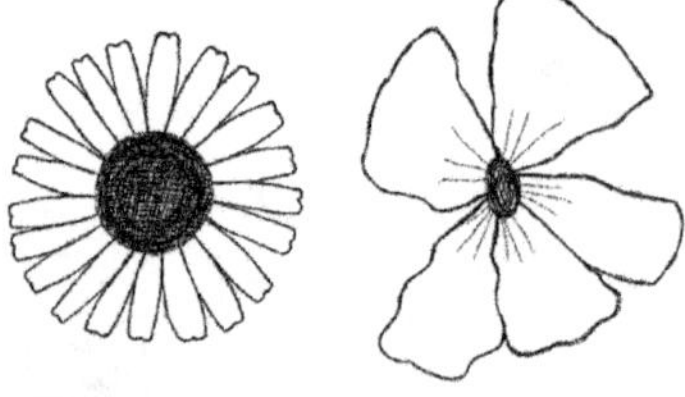

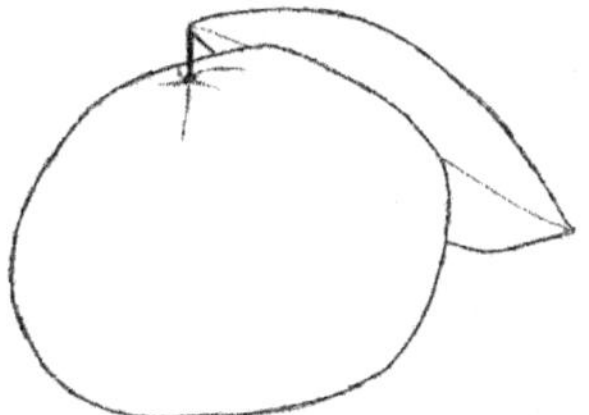

Naranja

From the fruit recognized by our state

To a bird's breast that resembles our name.

From gemstones and sunsets that catch my eye

To flowers that reach up toward the sky.

From vegetables we incorporate into our diet

To felines we rescued and claimed on accident.

From just a color that has recently claimed relevancy

To not only our existence, but our residency.

Morado 

The color hiding in your veins—

A representation of your pain,

But it is also the pigment of your birth.

The gems and flowers of the Earth

Share with you the same hue.

Reclaim that beauty and reuse.

Take the recollections that are hurtful,

And focus on the pretty parts of purple.

Adventures

We are advancing as scouts of adventure.

I adore traveling these terrains with you.

We are expanding our experiences

And inspiring our peers with our instances.

These journeys bring joy and help us center.

I anticipate our next adventure no matter the avenue

Because I learn and love more with our travels,

And they alleviate life’s aches and hassles.

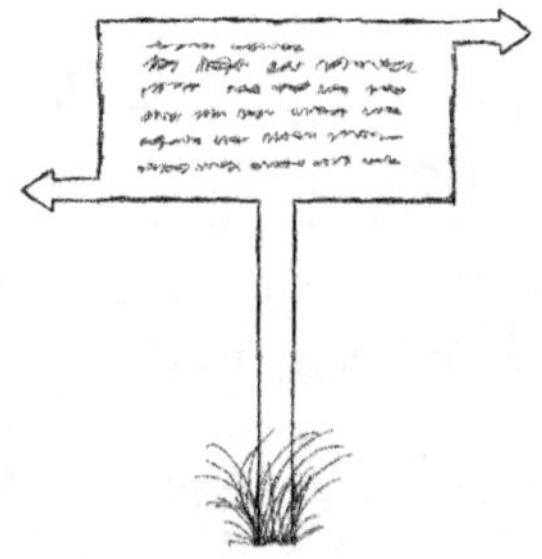

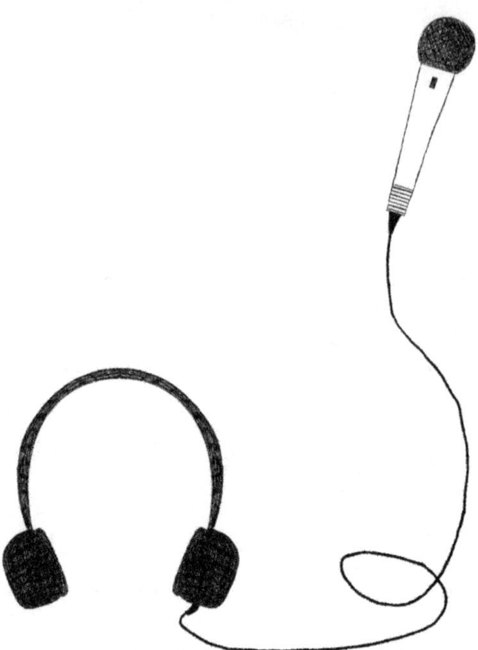

Musicians

Play me a song, and I will sing along—

Communication in the universal language.

With your heartbeat in my eardrums,

We can create an inspired album of love.

Writing rhythms on sheets and with the keys—

We can convert anything into an instrument.

Just allow your body to feel the music.

Let the frequencies leave an imprint.

Vibrations from our necks to our legs—

Dancing vocal cords until a cadence.

We continue to play these pieces to represent

The bond and love we hold as a testament.

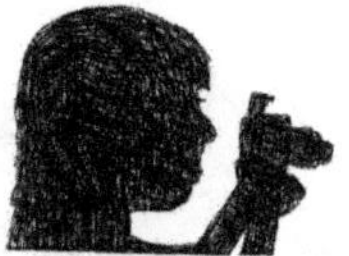

Photographer

She captures fragments of the world to display in her albums.

She may be fragile at times, but she finds pieces of peace in her pictures.

She keeps these copies in her pocket to access at any moment at the touch of a thumb.

She has a vision that others cannot envision, yet cannot see her own worth.

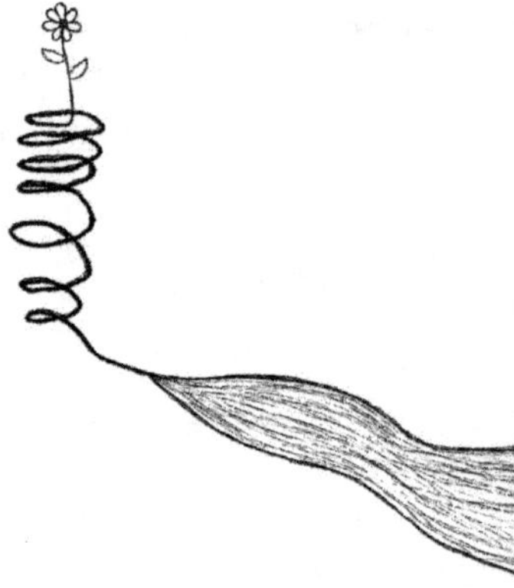

Springs

Into another adventure, we spring.

We can visit the natural springs.

Maybe we can go in the spring?

I hope we will, even with rusted springs.

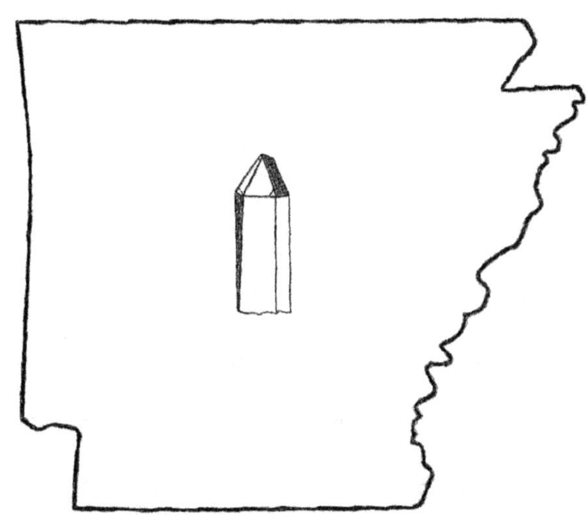

Arkansas, the Natural State

I could see us living here.

It feels like home but with nuance.

It may have a piece of my heart

Because this is part of my start,

But this place truly has an influence

That is beautiful and sincere.

With springs that could sear

And crystals to mine and flaunt.

On us, this land has left its mark.

Of all our adventures, when we depart,

It will be more difficult to be gone

From this pinned location on this great sphere.

Clay

Unearthing capsules of clay cushioning the crystals

While the scarlet clods color our clean skin.

With the sun casting rays captured by our faces,

We continue carving out the clumps in the mounds.

We continue to collect and keep our finds, then we haul.

It is addictive, but a healthy craving as well as therapeutic.

We could excavate until our knuckles fall into stasis,

But until we cannot, we will scour and sculpt these grounds.

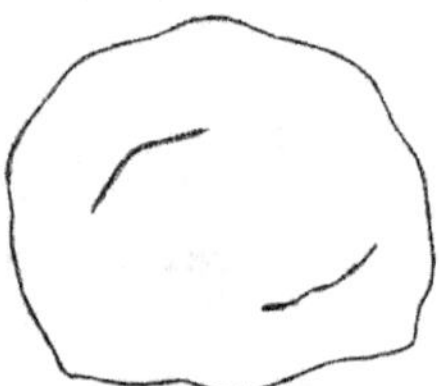

Mountains

Why wait to experience life while we are at our peak?

Especially when retirement and health are not guaranteed.

These treks through trails leave me revitalized though tired.

The scenery and greenery keep me excited and inspired.

My imagination flourishes as we walk through the mountains.

I love how we refuse to not climb through life regardless

Of others' negative perspectives or lack of understanding.

We crave Creation, and refuse to succumb to monotony.

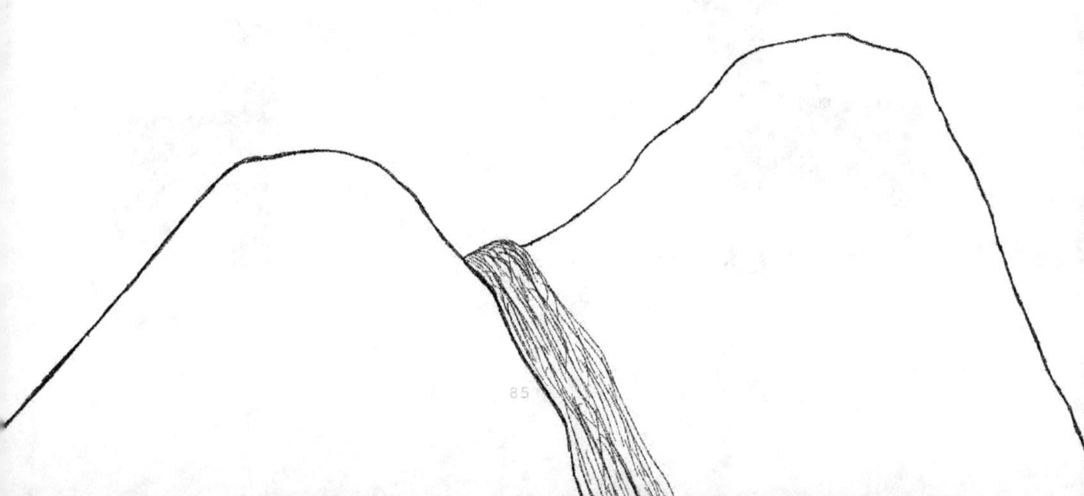

Dear, Deer

My dear little deer, we can graze the land for new adventures.

We can blaze the trails to find the wonders hiding behind the brush.

Even when our fur bristles while caught in the gaze of headlights,

It will be worth it to cut through the haze of routines and fears.

We can tuck our tails in this maze or we can navigate the timbers.

When we are stuck in a daze, we can remember the rush

That was once just a craze, but it is now our journey through this life.

Feel the inspiration as we look to the sunset creating a glaze over the meadow, my dear little deer.

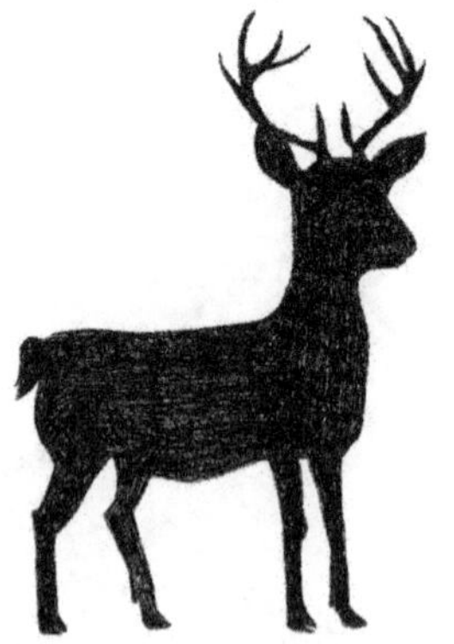

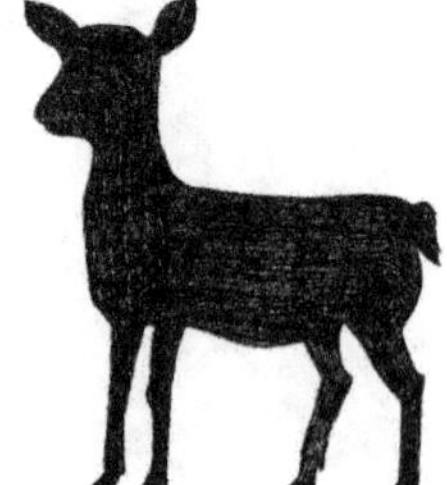

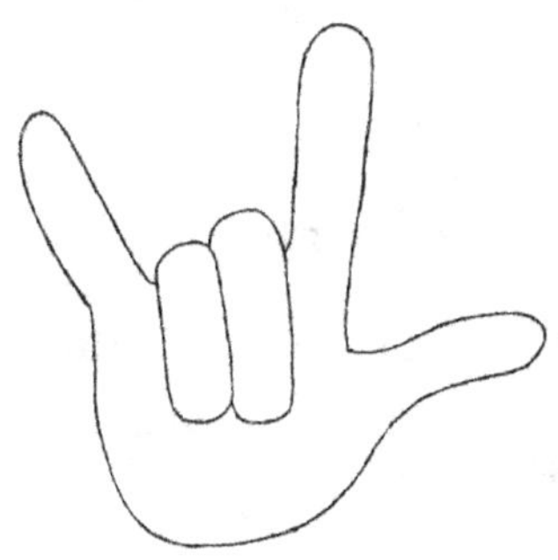

Private Display of Affection (PDA)

I apologize whenever I am cold and distant.

I cannot figure out why I cannot be consistent.

Though I cannot always keep the love physical,

It is ever-present in the realm that is mental.

It is certainly easier to display affection in privacy.

It removes the pressure that I presume is by society.

I always feel like I am awkward and inadequate,

And when I overthink, my sincerity becomes irrelevant.

Acts of Service

Caring for you is how I profess my love.

I want you to be comfortable and safe.

Whether I ensure your phone is plugged,

Or I let you rest while I fill the gas tank.

Sometimes it is through buying you a soda

Or simply cleaning out a pet's cage.

Sometimes making you a sandwich for lunch

Or purchasing CDs, vinyl records, or cassette tapes.

I try to clean the house and the Jeep because

I want you to relax, especially after being away.

I check your alarms so when you wake up,

Like a safety net, you will not be late.

I want to help you in your classroom as much

As I possibly can because you have a lot on your plate.

When you lack funds for vehicular repairs and such,

Without hesitation, I will wire money to your bank.

I want you to allow me to help you, though you are tough,

But remember, you have somebody to share the weight.

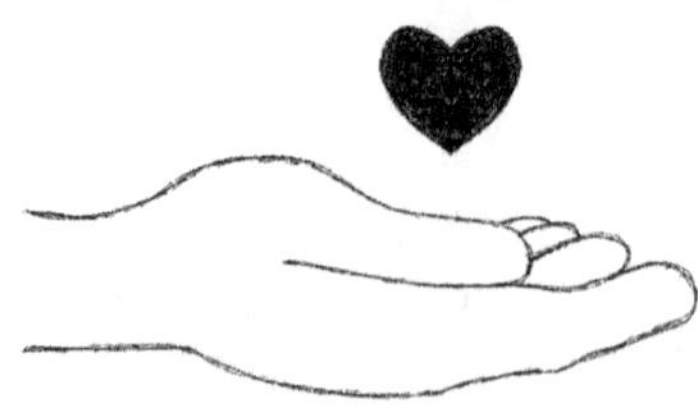

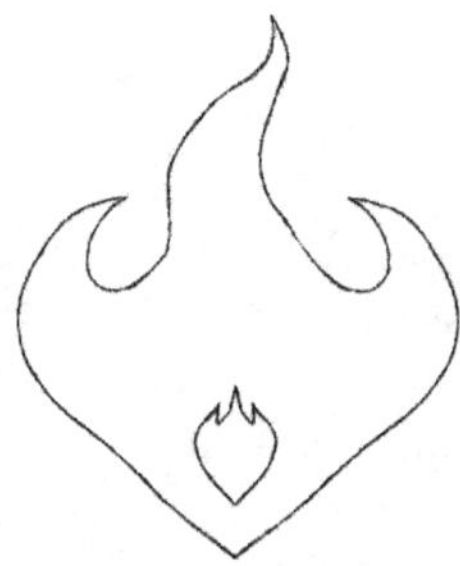

Chronic

I choose our love

Beyond any lust.

It is perpetually us.

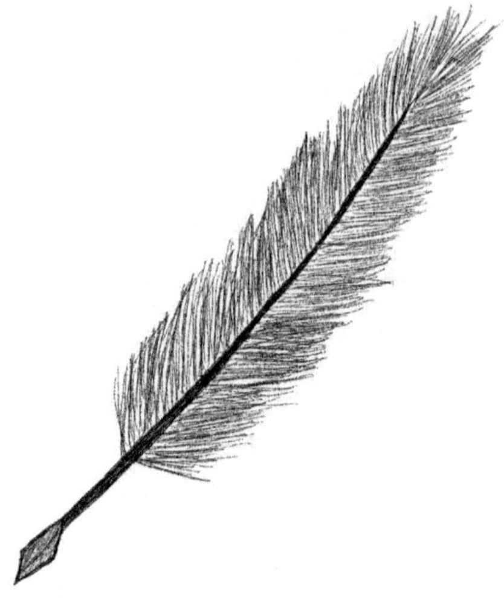

Poetess

She records her thoughts on the page

To detangle her brain and weave them

Into beautiful literature as a keepsake.

These poems are therapeutic as well as a token

Of triumph through tribulations and angst.

The words embellish like a tapestry or canvas

Filling her books and her notes as she decorates.

These letters are alluring as if they were painted.

Raw and powerful, living on the paper, they reign.

Lepidoptera

Over trials, we are scaling—
Winging through dust and stings.
You are like a butterfly—
Vibrant and beautiful.
I am like a moth—
Enriched by the night.
Maybe, however, I
Am the butterfly after all,
And cut from the same cloth,
You are the moth in flight.
I display my colorful wings
While you thrive in mystique.

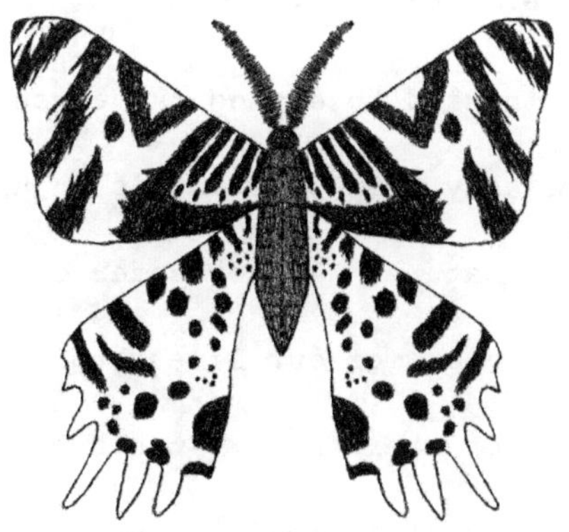

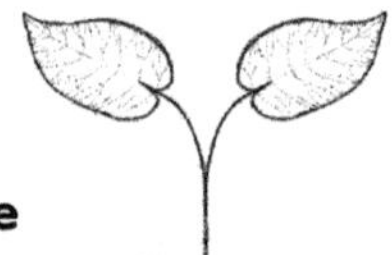

Our Nature Is Nature

We both tend to extend ourselves to nurture,

Especially when somebody is injured.

We are nature, whether safer or in danger.

As the years of our lives begin to taper,

No matter where we are taken on adventures,

What remains is that our nature is nature.

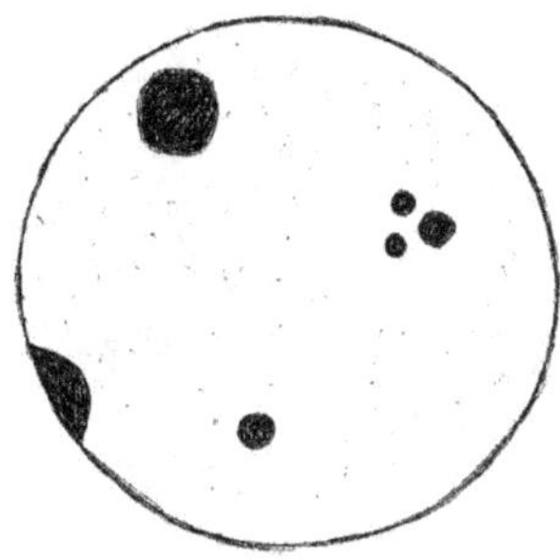
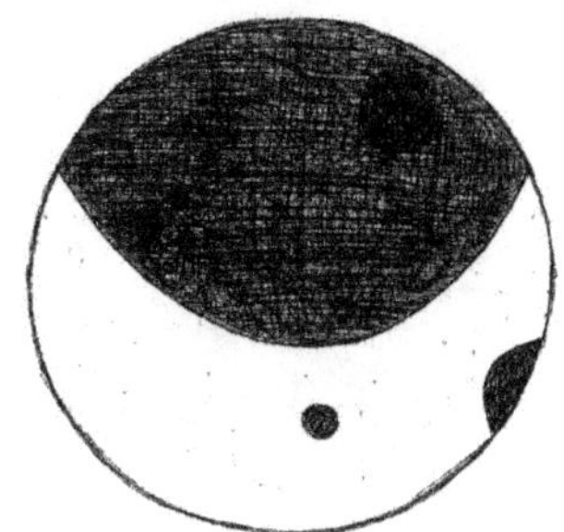

Nocturnal

You tell me you fall asleep better with me,

But it is difficult for me to accept the fatigue.

My body is lethargic, but my mind is stubborn.

My creativity lights up, but for rest, my eyes yearn.

I know I am actually diurnal, but I think I am nocturnal.

I just crave to create it all, especially at nightfall.

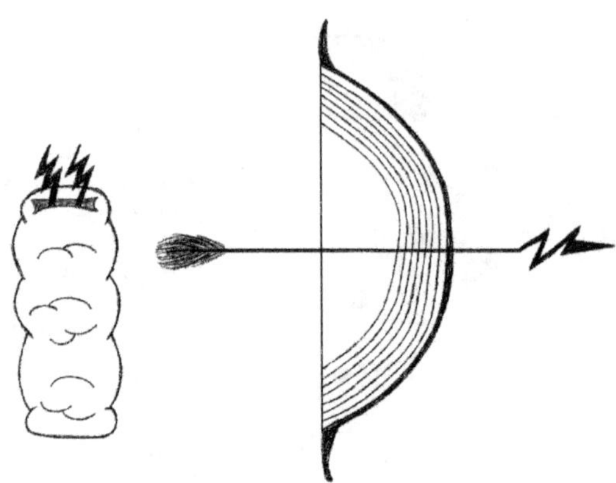

RainBows, Lightning Arrows, Cloud Quiver

The rainbows are only drawn

After the lightning arrows

Are pulled from the cloud quiver.

Tribulations, the rain may cause,

But it also helps us grow.

Storms can damage but also water.

Two Artists

We are two artists with different skill sets.

Different approaches that compliment

The piece that we both contribute to and share.

There are no wrong answers in this air,

But multiple pathways and solutions

To produce the same artistic creations.

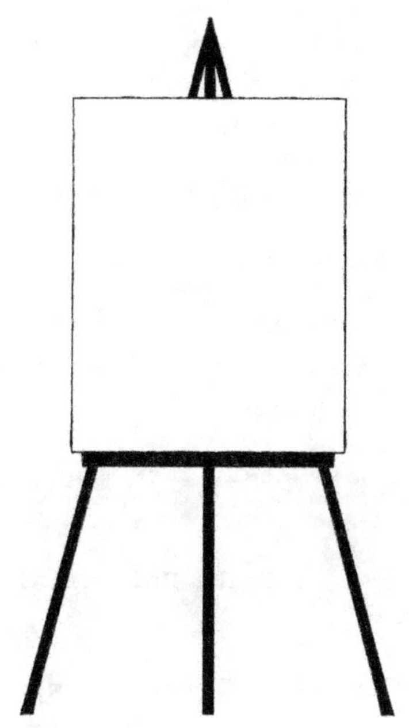

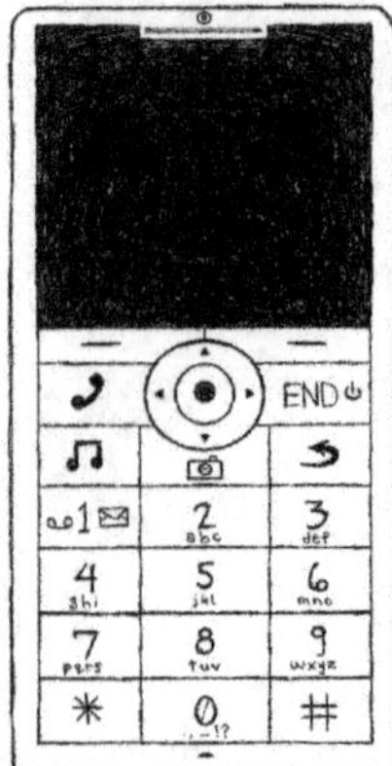

1996

What are the odds this year would begin both of our cycles around the sun?

How did we even end up meeting within this timeline?

I am likely biased, but our story feels so divine.

It is telling because our introduction was when we were a couple of kids.

Little did we know that back then is when it had all begun.

We already shared the area codes of our cell phones and landlines.

Now in a home with the same street address and zip code, we reside.

After all these years, my heart rate still shifts with every kiss.

With our guardian angels and The Holy Trinity watching over us,

We continue to make mistakes, learn, grow, recover, and thrive.

Together, on our adventures, we are not only alive, but we live life.

We will continue giving each other high-fives while dressed to the nines.

Island

When you look at me in adoration,

I cannot help but feel embarrassed.

I do not intend to reject your love.

I am uncomfortable with myself at best.

I feel like I am a deserted island,

And I feel where your eyes land.

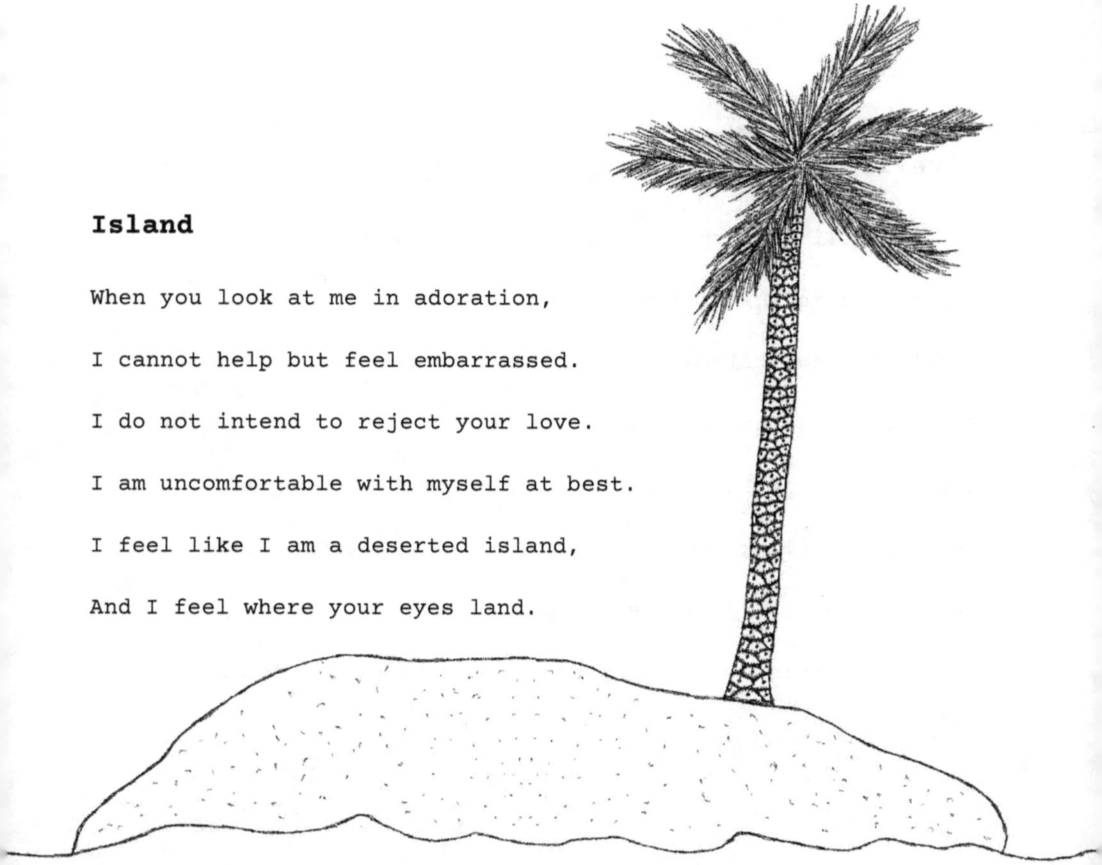

Fireflies/Lightning Bugs 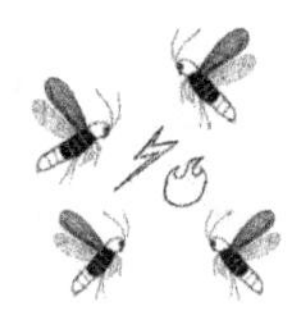

Fireflies light up the evening dusk into the night

Like twinkling night lights fluttering within reach.

Lightning bugs flickering in codes that narrate

The night must be writing a novel about us.

The contrast of intermittent flashes catches our eyes

As each orb blinks in patterns that give their speech.

We both seem to speak that language and can translate,

But only within that moment as they communicate our love.

Quality of Life

Days like these are the days I miss you most.

My heart is a cavernous chamber and you are the host.

My mind aches for your presence in my vicinity,

And my body cannot get to you as quickly as it wants to be.

Moments like these remind me that you improve my quality of life,

And I am so honored and proud to call you my wife.

Nights like these are when I am thankful you were there.

Your duties were on hold, so in my time of need, you were here.

You may be "obligated" to do so, but you did not have to.

You are "supposed to," but you have the will to refuse.

I have come to expect it, but I know it is a privilege, not a right.

Keeping you loved and respected improves my quality of life.

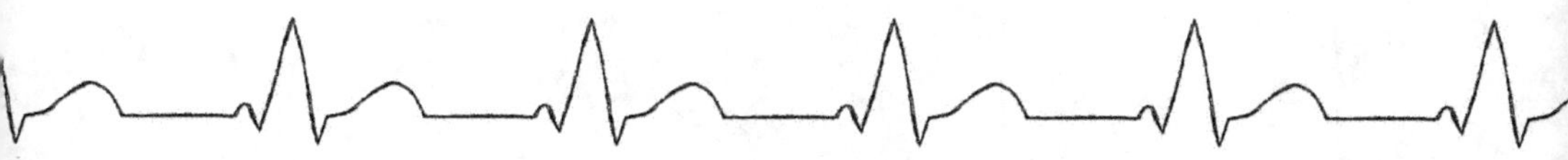

Rivers

I cannot bear to see rivers form from your eyes,

But instead a river in a forest with a mountainous background.

I want to be a part of the river rushing through your veins

Because being together allows our hearts to create rapids.

Then, when the view soaks in, I want a reprise.

We can discover a new river that enhances profound

Emotions within our hearts and in our brains

While we exist in harmony while the waters sing ballads.

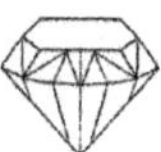 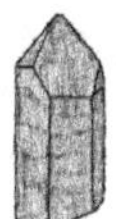

Diamond and Amethyst

We are both strong, but I forget that sometimes you can be fragile.

I am not the diamond I should be, and your colors are so deep.

I apologize for when I mishandle and treat you like gravel.

I only want to dig you out when you are buried in anxiety.

We can polish each other and complement each other's sparkle.

I intend to care for you better, value you more, and be more loving.

Foraging and Forging

Though I fail to acknowledge it as often as I should,

I want my appreciation for your care to be documented and understood.

I should not feel guilt for your loving acts,

Yet I feel like a daily burden on your back.

The gratitude I have for all the chores you complete every single day

Cannot be accurately depicted nor properly thanked.

As I attempt to match the level of your labors of love

With what I can provide, I know that it will never be enough.

I know we will continue to gather the pieces of life to write the story

That we want for us while we hone who we want to be.

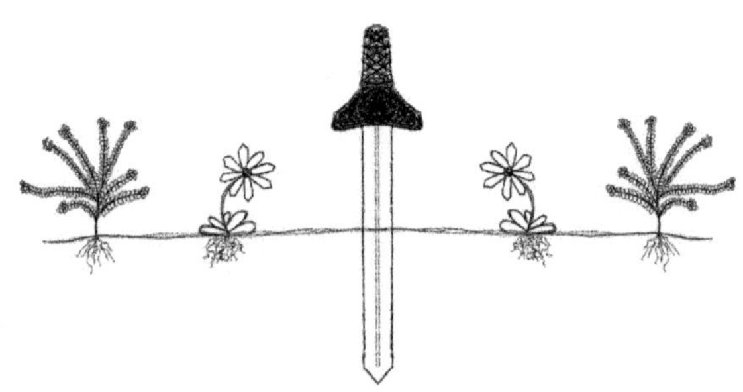

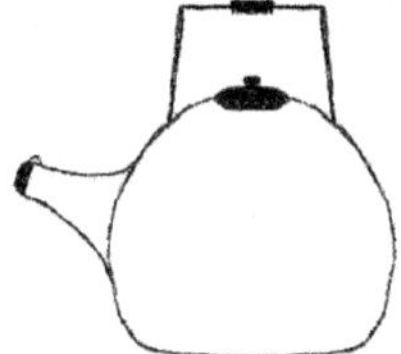

Sweet Tea

You are so sweet to me.

I could drink you up daily.

Your eyes are like glasses of sweet tea.

They are warm yet cool as well as comforting.

When I look into them, it is a remedy.

Whether you are hot or cold, I will still drink.

Servant's Heart

I yearn to serve you.

I will assist in your classroom.

I will replenish your gasoline,

So you can relax in safety.

I will clean the house

To surprise my spouse.

I will buy you outrageous gifts

That you would assume are myths.

I will labor in the dead of night

To make your morning bright.

I know I lack in physical touch,

But this is the language that speaks my love.

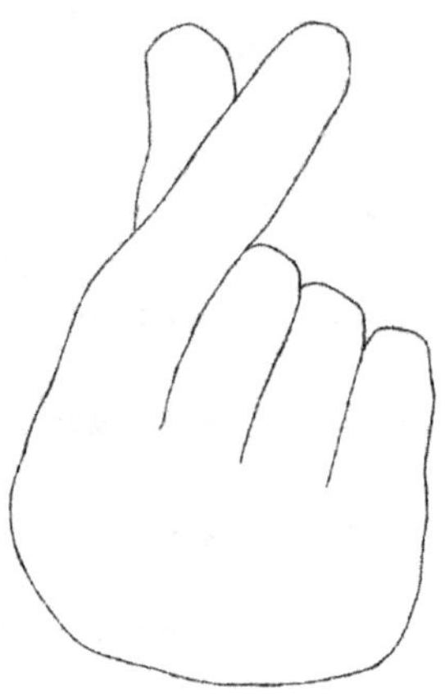

Zephyrs in the Sylva

Can we escape the tragedy that is life in this state?

I know it is improper to say that I cannot wait for Heaven,

And I know I will, but why must it be beyond the grave?

Maybe we can vanish to another dimension?

If not for you, I would have already abandoned this place.

Take me to where the goldenrods bloom in the sunset,

And the breeze whispers poetry to the trees and lakes.

Let us leave Earth, and travel to our secret forest——

A place where warmth is constant, and grief has no stake.

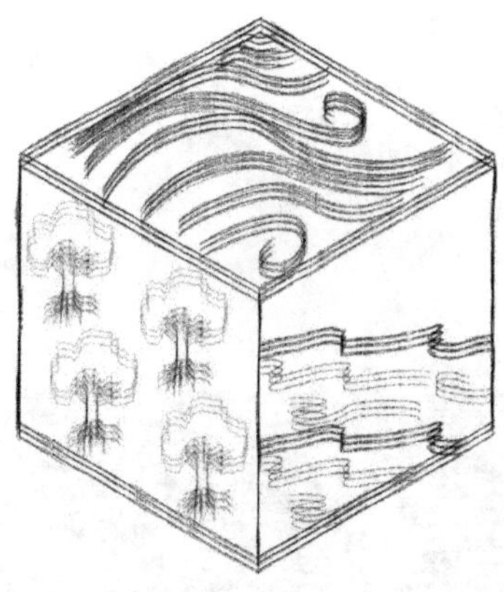

Gore/Gorgeous/Gorges

In this world filled with gore without justice,

You provide relief because you are gorgeous.

We thrive in trenches because we pretend they are gorges.

Not only on the surface, but through the gore,

You are more than I could ever bargain for

Though abrasions may leave you sore.

Phthalo

We blend together to make a color that is indescribable.

We enhance any palette that we are introduced to.

We produce the rawest and rarest of hues.

What we create is not something that is erasable.

Our pigment is rich, but not as appreciated by untrained eyes.

We compliment many shades in unconventional ways,

And those we touch absorb our stain.

“Until death do us part” is the oath—our hearts are forever dyed.

Grounding

When I start to drift into obscurity,

You are my tether.

When I begin storing too much electricity,

It is the release you inspire.

When I get struck by life's lightning,

You help put out the fires.

When my roots are exposed and wearing,

You are my gardener.

Whenever I go astray and need grounding,

You are there to help weather.

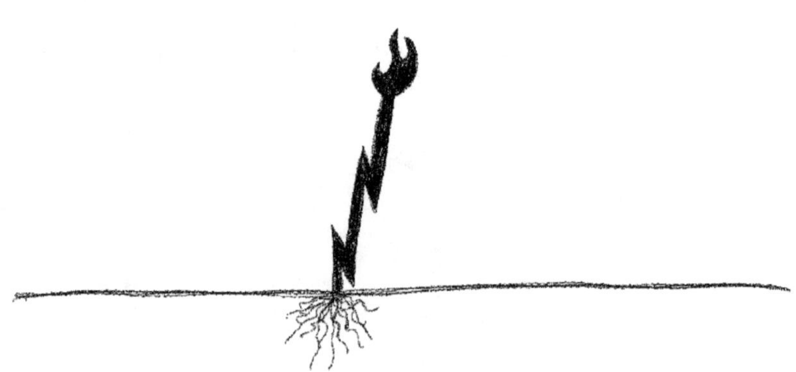

From February To April

We can pretend that your birthday is a national holiday,

And that it is actually you that everybody celebrates

Because you are my world—my city—my nation.

You alone are my everlasting vacation.

As for me, can we pretend that resurrection day is a second birthday,

So I can occasionally share the day with Jesus on Easter holiday?

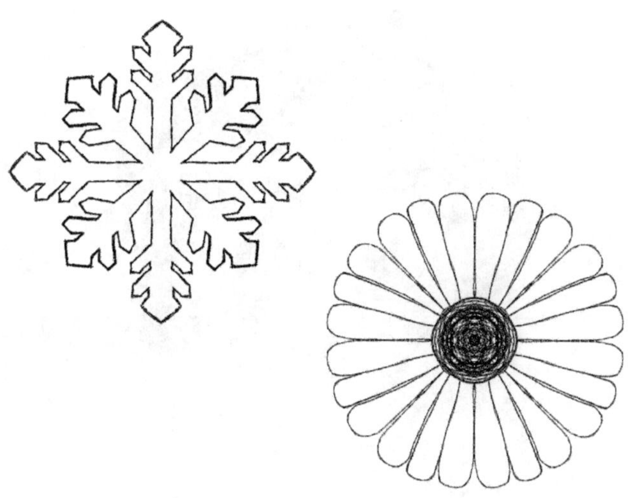

Comedian

When your sorrow is unbearable, I will prescribe you the best medicine.

I may not be a physician, but I endlessly aim to be your personal comedian.

You are my queen, and I am the jester who will meld your frown into a crown.

No longer in tears and fears will you be allowed to drown for I am your clown.

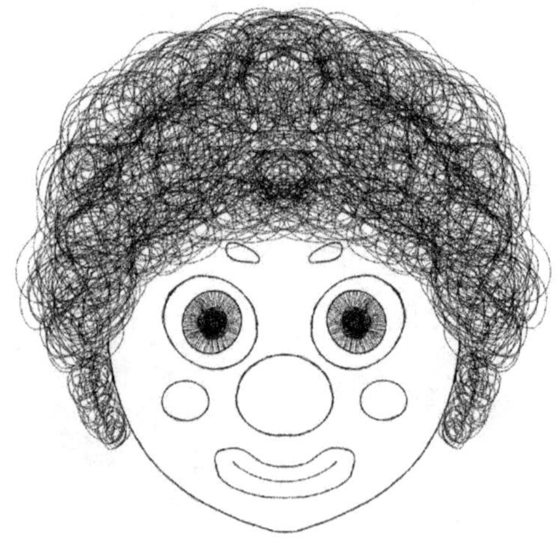

Fires of Rage, Waters of Sorrow

You say it upsets you when I am mad.

I say it upsets me when you are sad.

I do not mean to lose control in anger.

I fear that it will put you in danger.

There was hope for me that with age,

I would learn to become less enraged.

I have noticed your waters of sorrow

Douse my fires of rage from all to zero.

You periodically drown in your waters.

I intermittently am engulfed by my fires.

I need to learn to activate suppression,

While you learn to navigate depression.

Our emotions are separate oceans—

Maybe a fiery lake and a poisonous potion.

I am sorry when my flames cause pain

And sorrow, and I pray you are okay.

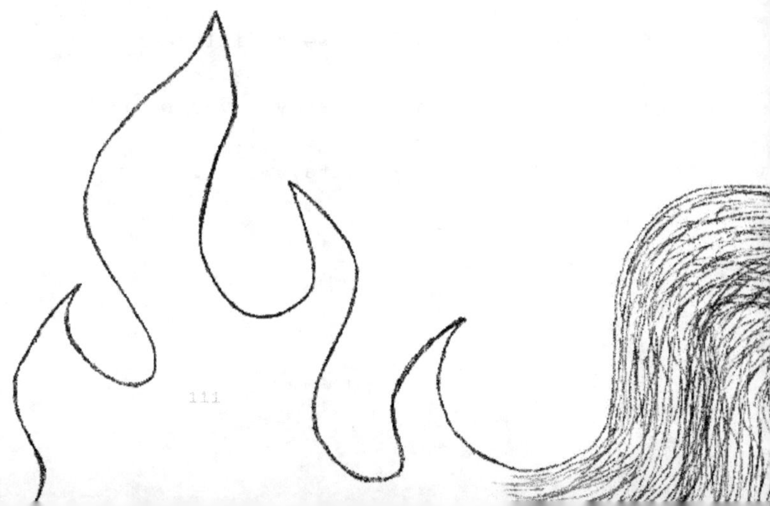

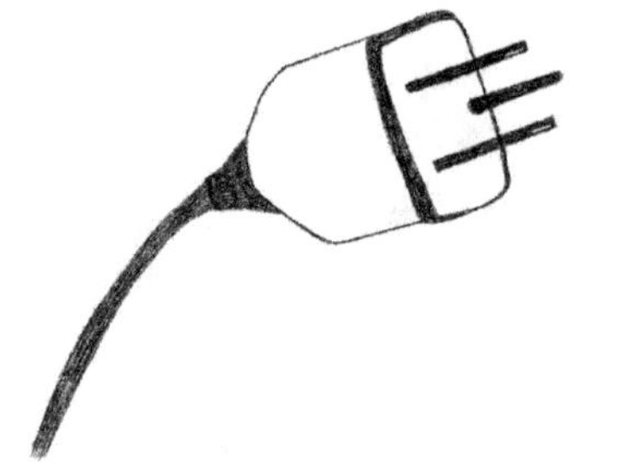
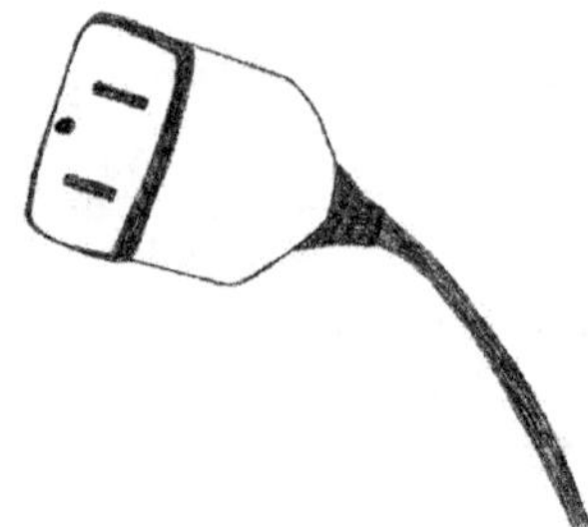

Opposites Attract

When one of us creates an outline, the other shades it in.

We are always drawing each other in and holding each other together like magnets.

When one is weary, the other has the strength.

When one is anxious or depressive, the other is on an opposite wavelength.

We are at different ends of the color palette

Which allows us to paint the town in a full spectrum.

We fill in each other's gaps whenever we begin to sink.

If one of us is hollow, we refill each other's ink.

Whenever my ions are negative, yours are positive,

And when they are opposite, we help one another charge them.

Opalized

We create the conditions for each other to sparkle.

What we have reminds me of a precious opal.

We are most vibrant when we are together.

You bring out my best tones, and I enhance your lovely colors.

Though sometimes you or I can be brittle,

We care for each other through big or little.

Over time, we have accumulated small fractures,

But we know how to appreciate each other.

We have a special ability to colorize any troubles

To transform them into something beautiful.

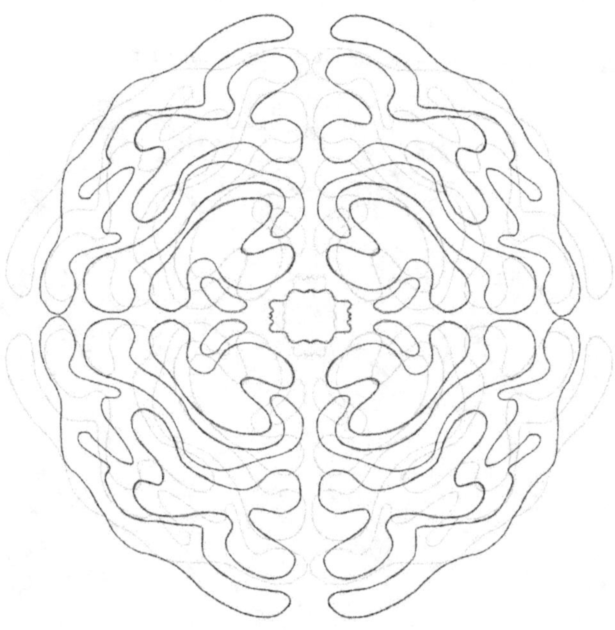

Crystalline

To me, you are crystalline.

You are sturdy yet fragile.

With me, you are translucent.

You are also multifaceted.

You are rare and magnificent.

You are like a precious gem.

Phoenix

You may have been burned,

But you will always return.

From all of your fear and hurt,

In your arsenal are lessons learned.

Ashes, like confetti, settle beneath your wings

As you rise and achieve your dreams.

Though you never know what tomorrow brings,

You are somebody who can accomplish anything.

Lucky 

I know you have had your unlucky moments,

But overall, with "luck," I think you are blessed.

You are so calculated—I am not convinced of dumb luck.

Each plan or scheme of yours is hand-plucked.

Waterfalls

I know how much you love waterfalls,

But you do not have to create your own.

You can keep the beautiful caverns

Of your face dry, and we will find

Nature's wonders to put us in awe.

Let your worries wash away with the flow

As you stand and admire the ferns.

Your best natural remedy is a hike.

Bioluminescence

You have a natural tendency to glow in the darkness—
Always finding your way no matter how dim.
When those around you are bland and grim,
You have a way about you to spark this
Radiance that creates warmth and bliss.

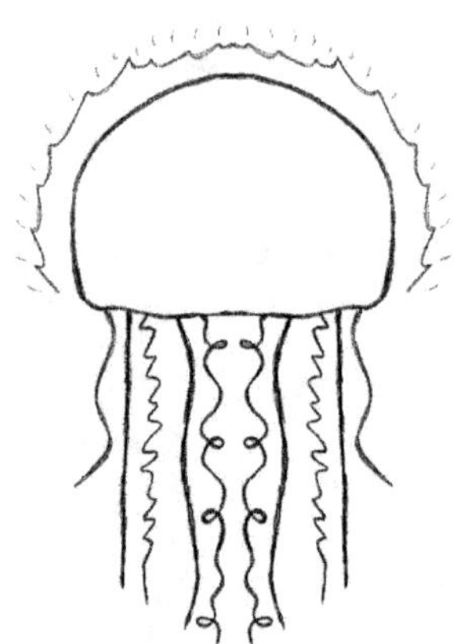

The Cats

Can we run around like little kids?

Maybe we can pretend to be kittens.

Carefree and spontaneous—kindred spirits—

I aspire to once again be like that.

If only we could reincarnate and go back.

For now, we can learn lessons from the cats.

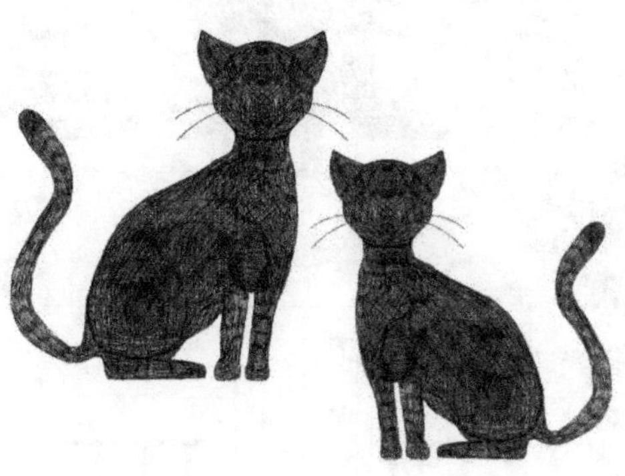

Off the Grid

I know if you had a chance to leave,

I could find you under the canopy—

Beneath the palette of painted leaves

Just before you can see the skeletons of the trees.

I know I could find you in a mythical forest

With the birds singing as you tend to your garden,

And after the day's work, you would rest in your cottage.

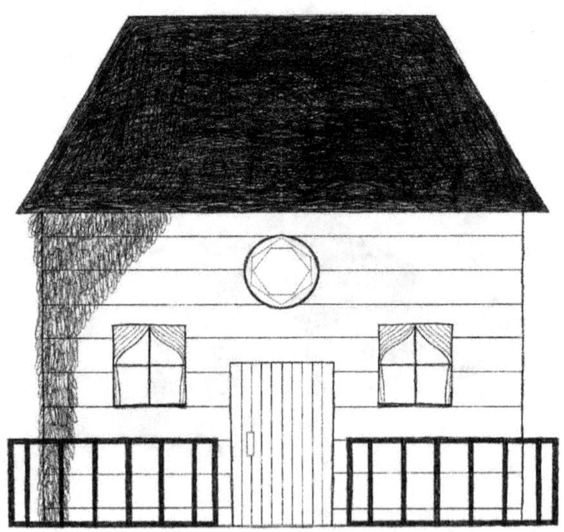

Proxy

I want to take care of you—

Physically and fiscally.

I love it when I impress you—

Mentally and sentimentally.

Through sickness and health

Or financial loss and wealth,

We will be each other's caregivers.

If one is down, the other will deliver.

It is comforting to confide in your love

Because you go beyond and above.

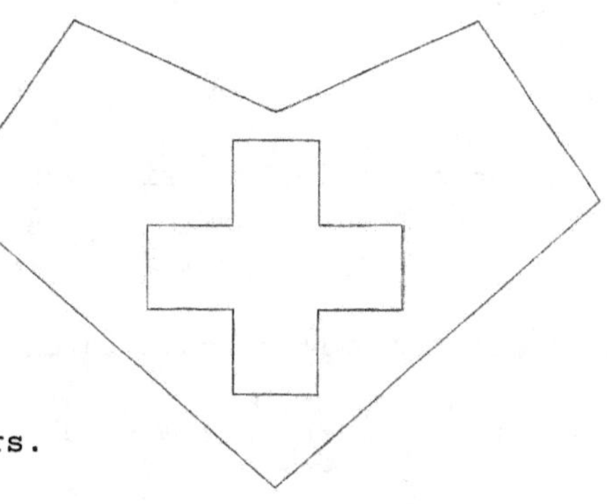

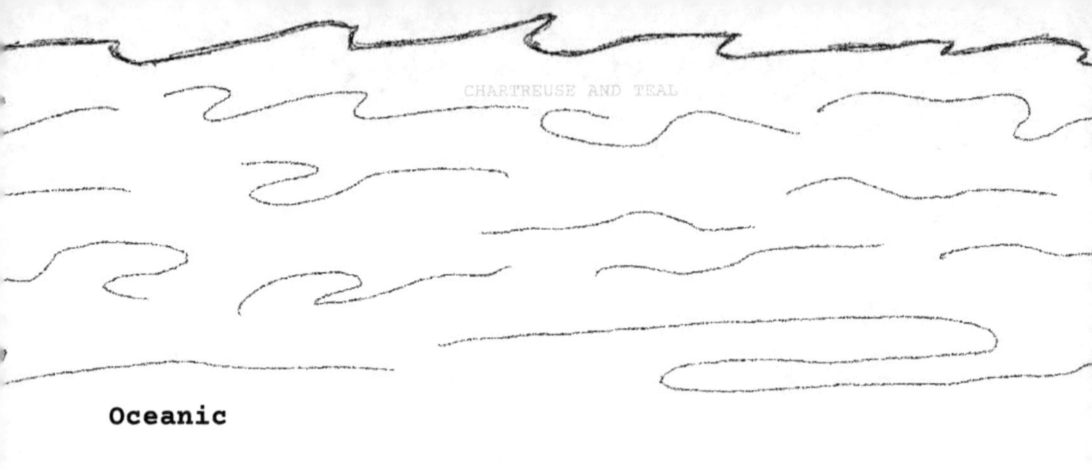

Oceanic

You are a true enigma, but not to me.

You are like an ocean, vast and deep.

Many drown, but those who are equipped

With skills or gills or flotation or ships

Swim with you and enjoy your waves.

We do not struggle, but with you, we wade.

Currents may try to pull me under from my toes,

But I will transition that into a dive into the throes.

I am with you through the thick and the thin—

Either way, with you by my side, I will swim.

Because of your mystique, I am always drawn to you,

Just as the tides push and pull as directed by the moon.

Though my mind has a tendency to panic,

Your stillness juxtaposed with power is oceanic.

Honey

Honey, you enhance my life so much.

You bring flavor and energy with your love.

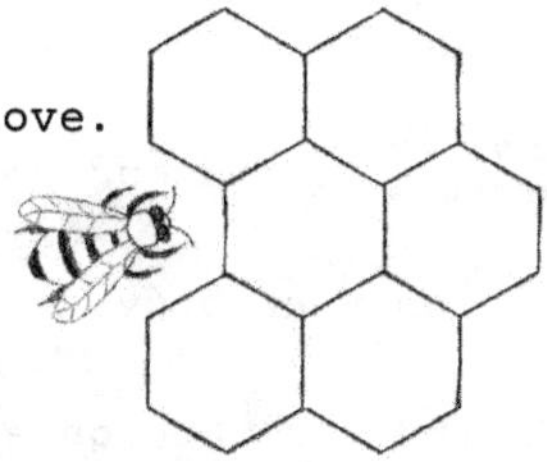

Can I be yours, and will you be mine

Forevermore and until the end of time?

A love like ours will never expire or taste bad.

Our shelf-life is what they all aspire to have.

Maybe it is something about the birds and the bees.

You pollinate my heart; you are sweet like honey.

Firearm

I know you can handle your own,

But I am always ready to strongarm

Anybody who crosses you incorrectly.

I know I am a spitfire ready to throw blows,

And you are tactful and deliberate like a firearm.

Together, we are a force like an army.

Consider me a loaded gun ready to overthrow

Any attack on your body, mind, soul, or heart.

I will defend you through any battle or siege.

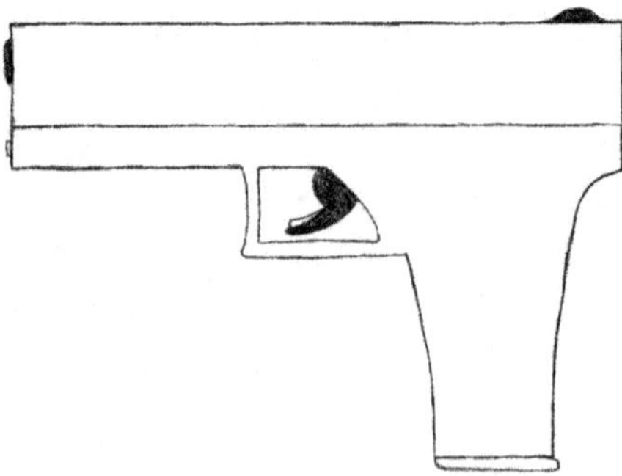

Sunflower or Moonstone or Sunstone or Moonflower

You are soft and beautiful like a flower.

You can bloom wherever you please.

I am rough and rigid like a stone.

I can get so cold and so mean.

You are cool and quiet like the moon—

A mysterious force with a gleam.

I am hotheaded and formidable like the sun—

Whether in jubilation or frustration, I will beam.

These attributes may be solar,

Or perhaps they may be lunar,

But ultimately they compliment each other—

Filling in the spaces for one another.

The rays of the sun or the rays of the flower

Both have their place and their own power.

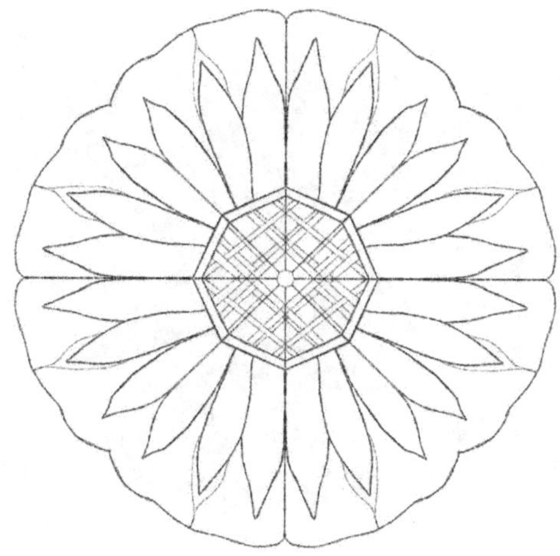

Blue-green

I apologize when I crumble, and when you witness it too.

Why is it that we never seem to be able to get ahead of the dues?

Whenever we are in the midst of calamity, that is the next tragedy's cue.

Because of these unfortunate situations with the green, I am blue.

Being young and green leads to missteps that develop into sagacity.

Though, as our youth begins to flee, I cannot help but feel a sort of envy

Of our younger selves and the generations that come before me.

Time may be fleeting, but I feel more alive and free than previously.

It is confusing what I am feeling—all I can describe it as is blue-green.

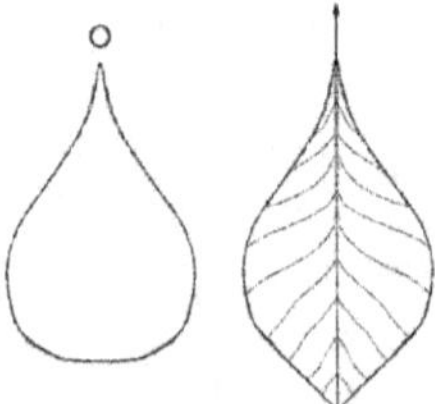

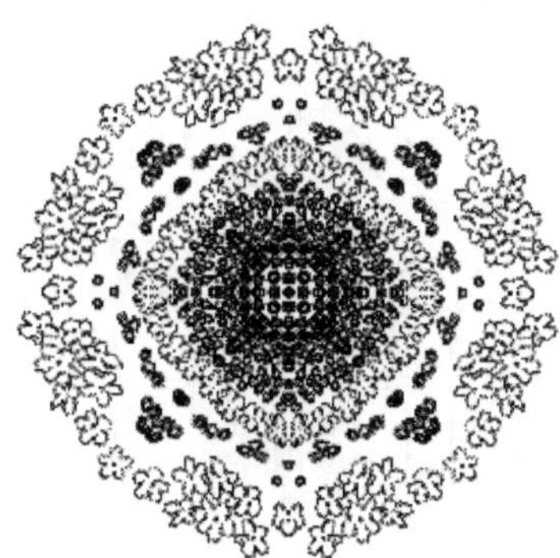

Medicine Bow

It is here that we can be still and rest.

Safe behind these walls we can heal.

We often hunt for adventure, but home

Is where we can be at ease and recover.

Through whatever sickness or stress,

We can be safe and warm together here.

Though our gift is to ability to roam,

It is nice to be at my quarters with my lover.

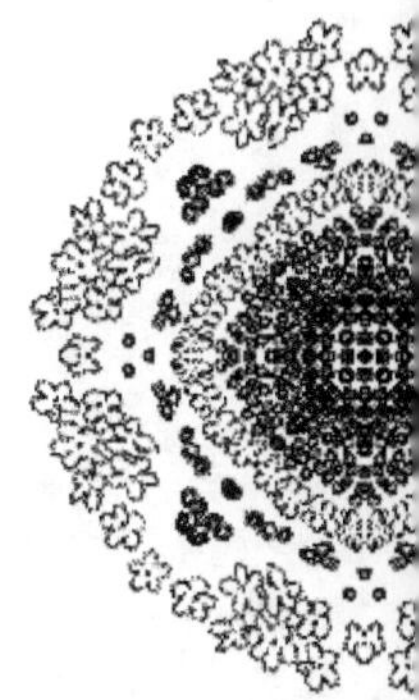

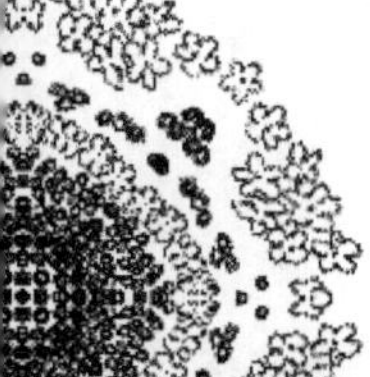

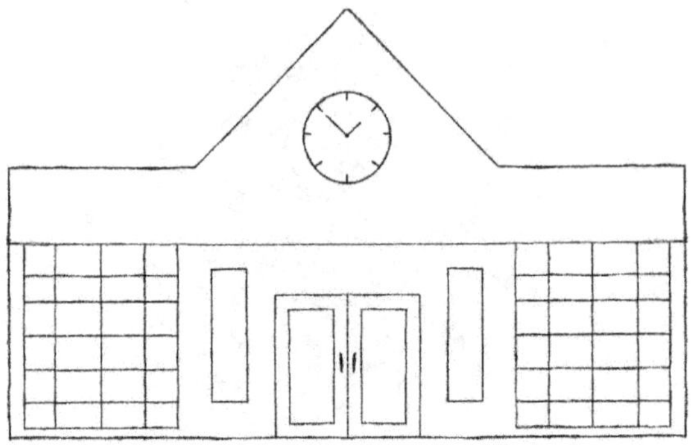

Students and Patients

We joke about the full moons and what is in the food

Whenever we have a difficult day with unruly people,

But what is really amusing are the parallels of our careers.

Even in our jobs, how are we so similar yet so different?

I suppose whether it's elders in a hospital or kids in a classroom,

Human beings begin and end in the care of other individuals.

There is always knowledge to share and learn as we steer

Them in the right direction—your students and my patients.

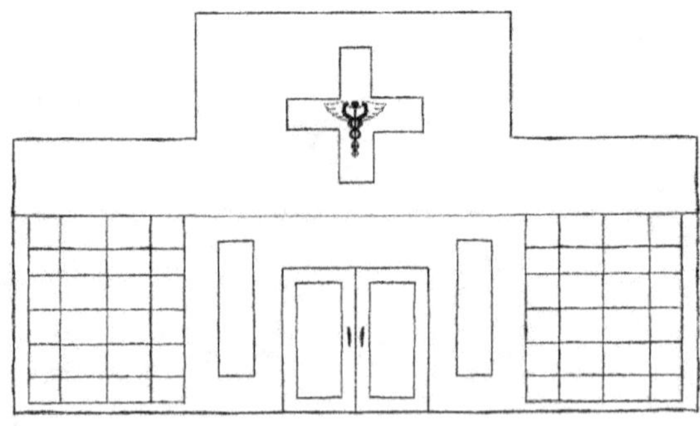

Wildfire

Sparks fly whenever we spend this time together.

You make my cold heart race and become warmer.

I do not, however, require the use of a fire extinguisher,

Though all of this heat does set my heart on fire.

It may get too hot and tiring, but when passion is burning,

Why would we stop this friction even if it creates a wildfire?

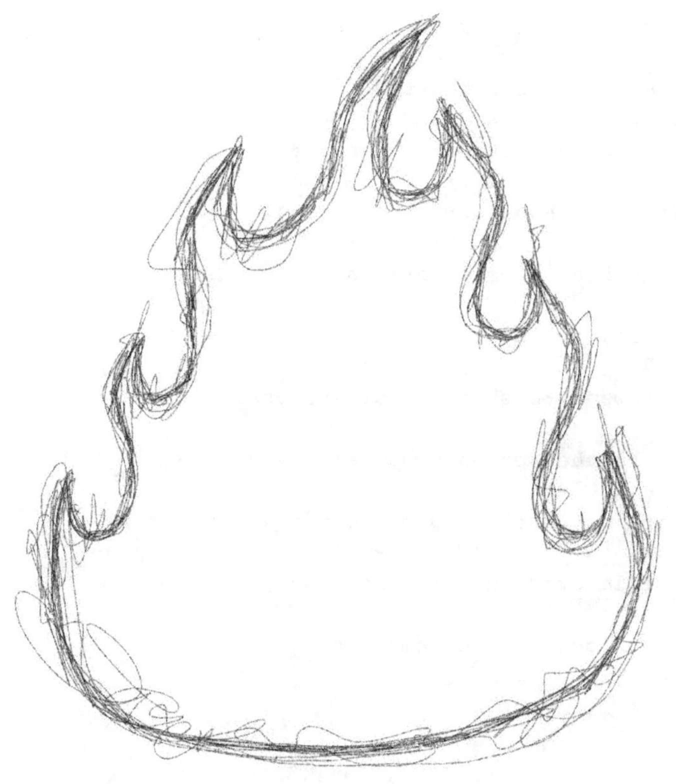

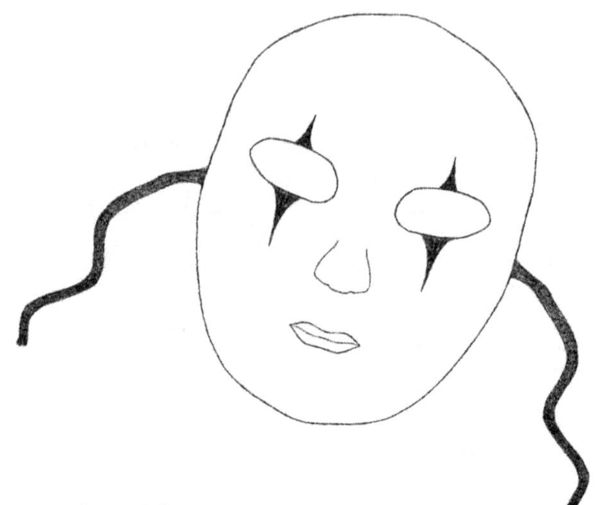

Actors

We both have mastered masking.

They are never aware if we are acting,

But we see each other's hearts.

We decipher the scripts—it is an art.

People think they know our true person,

But they only know a mere version.

Whether we play or get serious, we

Know what we want to show on our screens.

It is not like the movies, what we feature.

It is genuine but subtly more limited and blurred.

We allow a film over our presentation

To hide all of our damaged emotions.

Green Apple, Blue Raspberry

I may be sour, but you are sweet.

We are a power couple—a treat.

This love of ours may be niche,

But as it flowers, it is ideal for you and me.

I sit and scour my deficiencies.

Love between vowers is hard, soft, bitter, sour, spicy, salty, tangy, and sweet like candy.

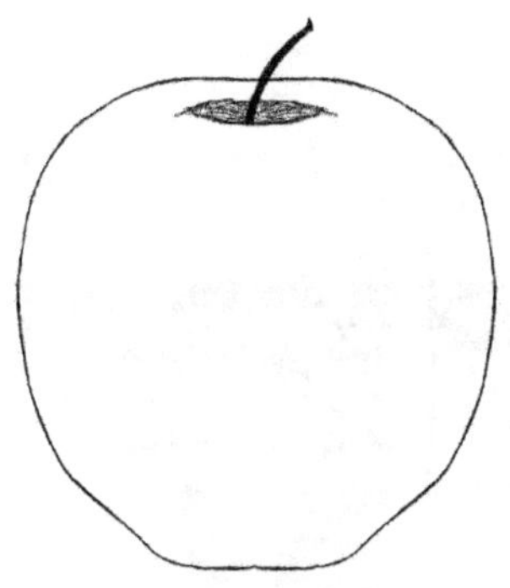

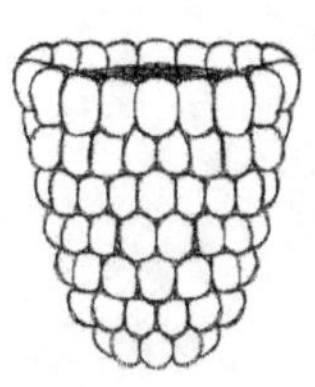

ZooFarm

We share a love for animals that is deeper than most.

Our warmth and compassion allow for us to be their host.

We fill our home with these beloved, rescued creatures.

People may not understand it, but we do—that is what matters.

I am forever grateful to have found somebody who also believes

In love and justice for anything that has a living heart that beats.

We have a full house now, but slots will open as they come and depart,

And as painful as it is, Heaven is their home but so are our hearts.

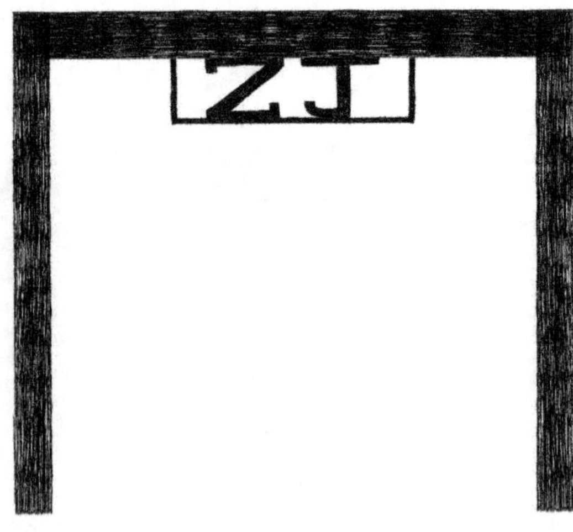

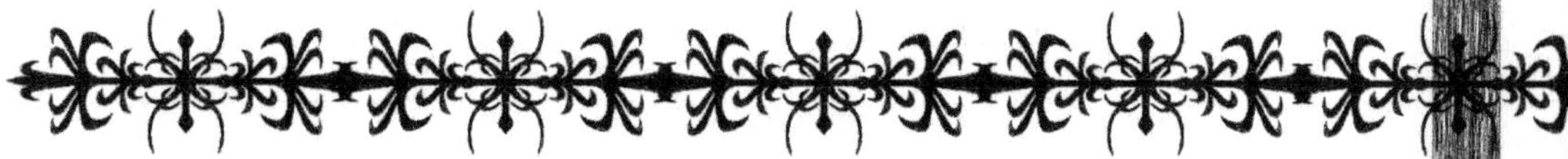

Gothic/Rustic

We live on a spectrum that is invisible to the untrained eye.

We dance between waves of darkness and a southern touch.

We cannot be completely understood or accurately defined.

We do not fit into a pattern or a mold—we are too complex.

We both have so much to offer and so many things on our minds.

We cannot be predicted or boxed in—when steadfast, we will not budge.

We have interesting architecture within our relationship that is divine.

We have styles that compare and contrast, and we create beauty from mess.

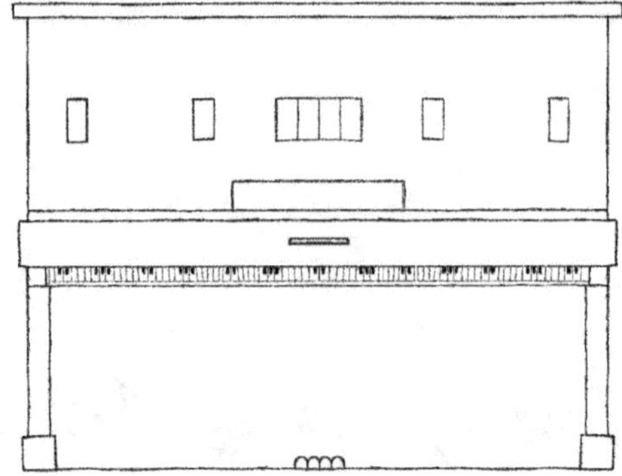

Piano and Guitar

As we strum each other's heartstrings,

We write and play a celestial melody

As we operate together in harmony.

We form a band in holy matrimony.

We are each other's fans during our symphony.

Each song decorates the air we breathe,

Telling the tales in tunes of our love story.

Even if my ears pop, know you are my rock endlessly.

We orchestrate these soundwaves deliberately.

The music we conduct is timeless and undying.

Our love is the psalm I will forever sing

As our hymns bring to Him the glory.

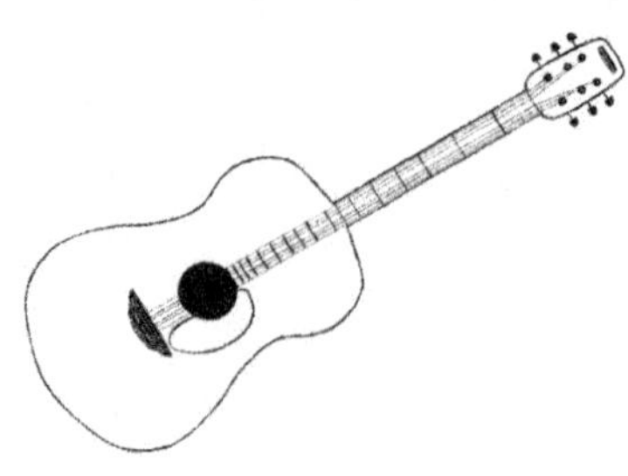

Bijou

Please, stop being so hard on yourself.

You are a gem—you are a jewel.

You are worthy and spectacular.

I would never just leave you on the shelf.

To your heart, you need not be so cruel.

With an abundance of skills, you are not lackluster.

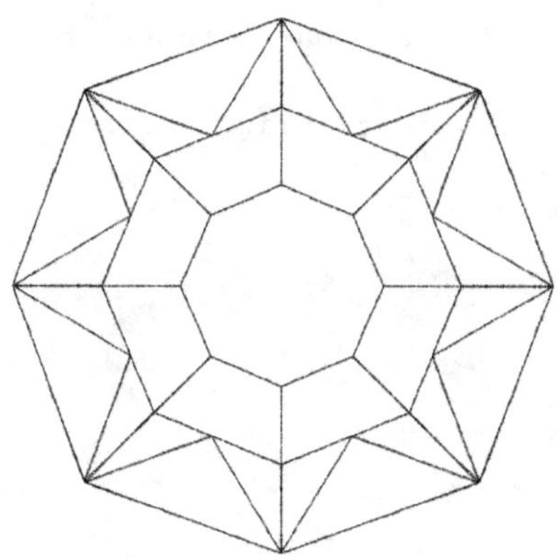

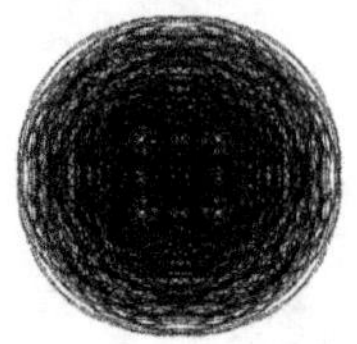

Period.

I cannot bear to witness your suffering.

If there was a way I could squelch your pain,

Or if I could carry that burden for you, I would trade.

How you feel may be beyond my understanding,

But if there was more I could do, I would not hesitate

To alter that state and change those traits.

I ache with the desire to bring you healing.

Melancholy Melody

While you stand next to me, I can sense your melancholy,

So let me hold you, and I will sing a melody.

As we dance to the rhythm of our heartbeats,

I see your smile emerge, and I know you are healing.

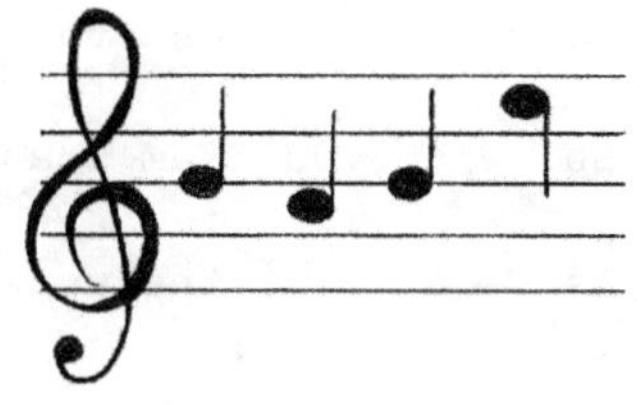

Falling under the Waterfall in the Fall

In these moments, the springs that feed my heart
create waterfalls

Reminding me of why I fell for you—I recall.

My emotions overflow and saturate my mind like
the colors of spring and fall.

On my own, I tend to feel so small,

But with you I am standing strong and tall.

As we gaze at the water under this overlook and
take in it all,

I realize that, like these waters, for you, I
will continue to fall.

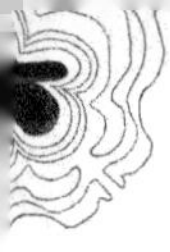
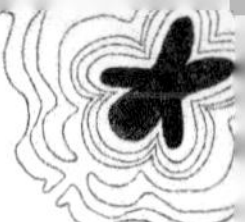

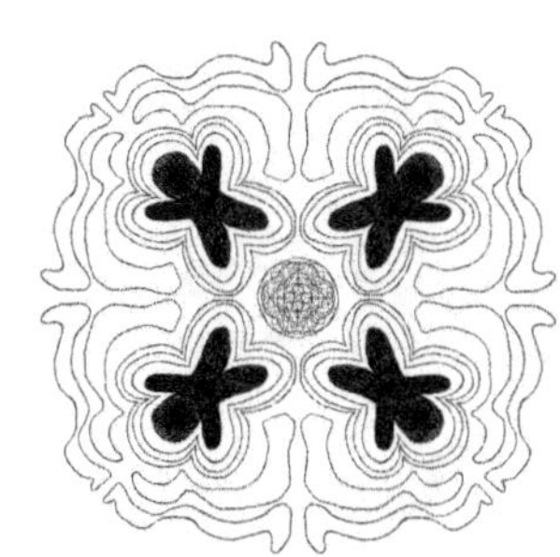

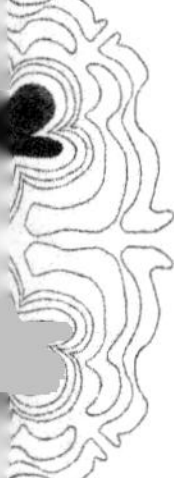

Aura

A spiritual gift we both seem to possess

Is the ability to exercise discernment.

We both can effectively detect

Somebody's mood or character with keen judgment.

Though we both have this extra sense,

That does not mean you are exempt

From my utilization of it for your emotions.

You can claim being "fine" or remain silent,

But I can feel when you are burdened.

All I want is to provide rehabilitation

And ease your mind, but I feel useless.

I promise to give my best effort to lift your spirits

And shift the colors of your ambience.

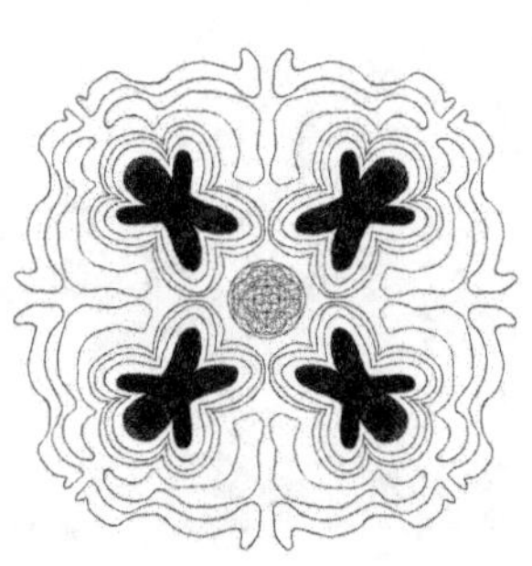

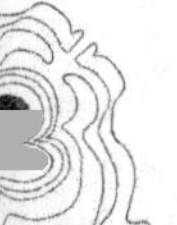
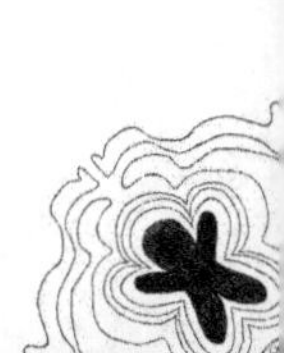

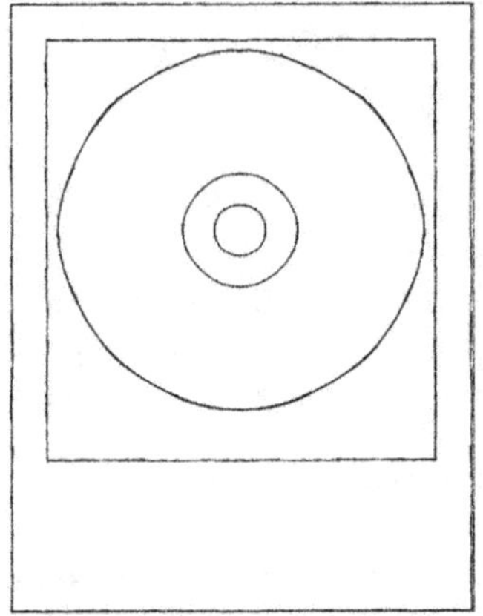

Albums

I document my emotions with words and sounds

While you express yours with images floating in the cloud.

The mediums we upload our art through may differ,

But the parallels between us are to be considered.

I curate soundscapes with borrowed noise in the airwaves,

And you capture landscapes utilizing light's wavelengths.

We are constantly creating albums for others to enjoy

While simultaneously constructing our own joy.

Ambidextrous

I am your right-hand man as well as your biggest fan.

You and I may be out of left field, but we can wield

Any tool or weapon because together we are ambidextrous.

I know I am not always right, but I do want to understand why.

Having you is my privilege, not my right, and I am delighted.

Before, you were left on your own, but at my side, you will not be alone.

When our hands interlock as a unit and our prayers align, we strengthen.

Together, we are centered with a stronger grip, and we bring balance to each other.

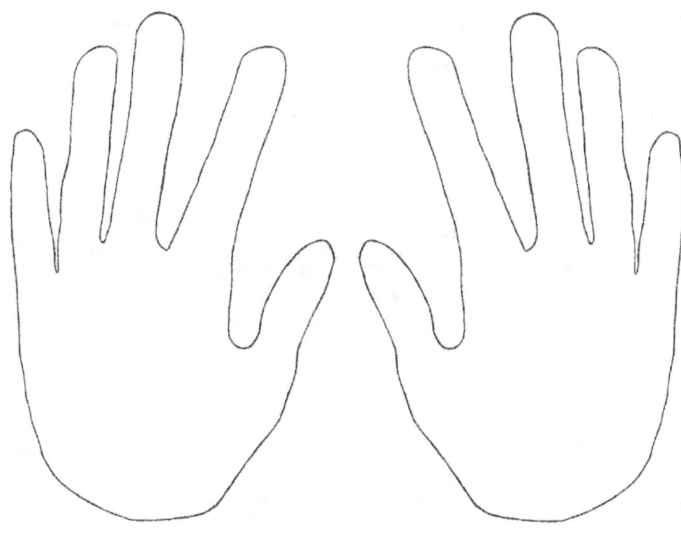

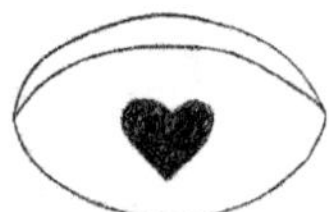 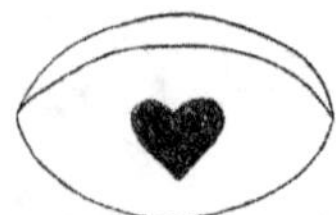

Eyes Do; I Do

Why are you unable to perceive yourself the way my eyes do?

You must understand that there is a reason I agreed to the "I do."

I want to mend you by wrapping my arms around you.

Similarly to how my pupils are encircled by green and gray-blue.

If I could create a pair of teal-tinted glasses that allow us to share my view

Of you, maybe then you would understand with those lenses too.

Where the Colors Lead Us

The fresh spring greenery plays off of the sun's beams

To create chartreuse light gleams after a storm so heavy.

As the pale blue sky fades into a deep teal, cloudy night,

We reflect on life and embrace this quiet time.

I wonder when and where we will adventure next,

And what all we will see on that forthcoming quest?

Maybe we will find an emerald pond beneath a canopy of trees as it hides——

Or cheerful voices surrounding a blazing bonfire with a core of sapphire.

Regardless of where our travels lead, whether just our backyard or the deep sea,

We will always make special memories that we will treasure and keep.

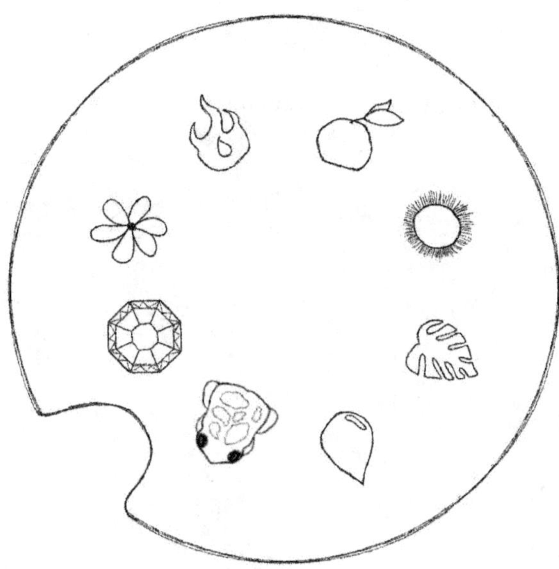

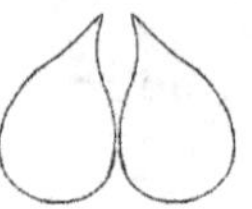

I Apologize

I am aware that your intention was to be helpful,

And I apologize that I reacted like a hellion.

I truly am making the effort to correct this behavior,

And I do not want my anxiety to wreak havoc.

All I desire is to be the reason your heart is full,

Not for you to walk upon eggshells and have trepidation.

It is a rewarding feeling to give you my hand for favors.

I never want you to wear pain, but only to feel loved.

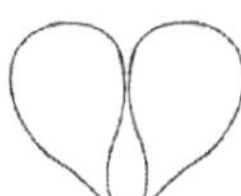

Labradorite Eyes, Opal Smile

Lean on me whenever you are in need.

I crave to help you whenever you thrive or bleed.

When my labradorite eyes meet your opal smile,

We create an iridescent scene that flashes and shines.

You do not have to figure it all out on your own.

I am always willing to assist, so you are not alone.

We may be alienated from the rest of society,

But we have each other to create our own country.

Together, we always create such beautiful things,

So why not combine our colors to maximize our offerings?

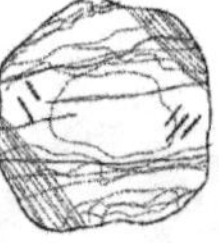
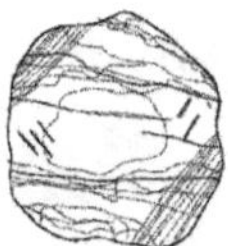
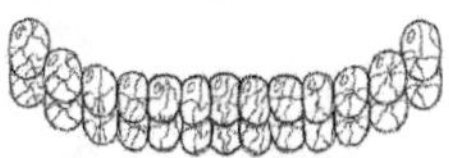

Canvas and Denim

I am like canvas—made of cotton or hemp or linen—

And you can go with anything like denim.

I am constantly creating and ready to be repainted,

And you have the ability to blend with those rugged spaces.

You are a seamstress even when you seem stressed,

And I wish you could muster the confidence to try new palettes.

I wish I could feel comfortable in this demographic.

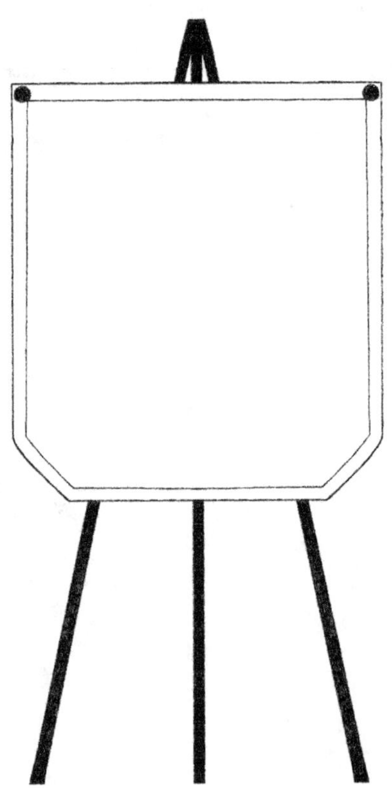

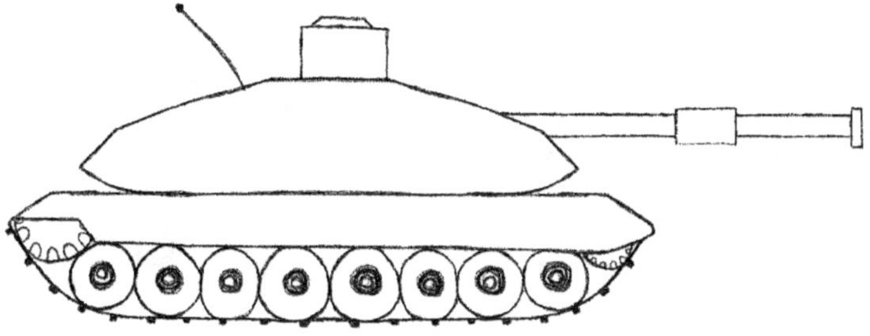

Army and Navy

You always have my back, and I have yours.

Together we are an incredible, unwavering force.

We fight for each other like soldiers in a war.

Land or sea—inland or on any shore—

Being with you, I could not ask for more.

Every loss and every victory deepens our lore.

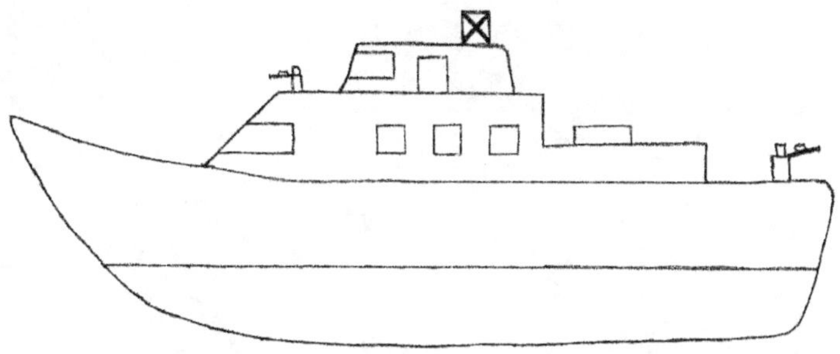

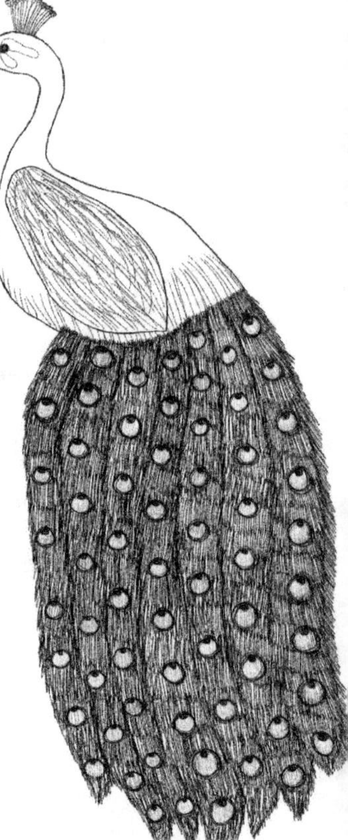

Verde y Azul…Blau und Grün

She is beautiful, fun, wise, and intelligent.

My thoughts are painted with her.

Two colors that perfectly compliment—

We could colorize the entire Earth.

That is how we are—amazing and vivid.

We are a natural wonder together

Like plants and water or oceans and forests.

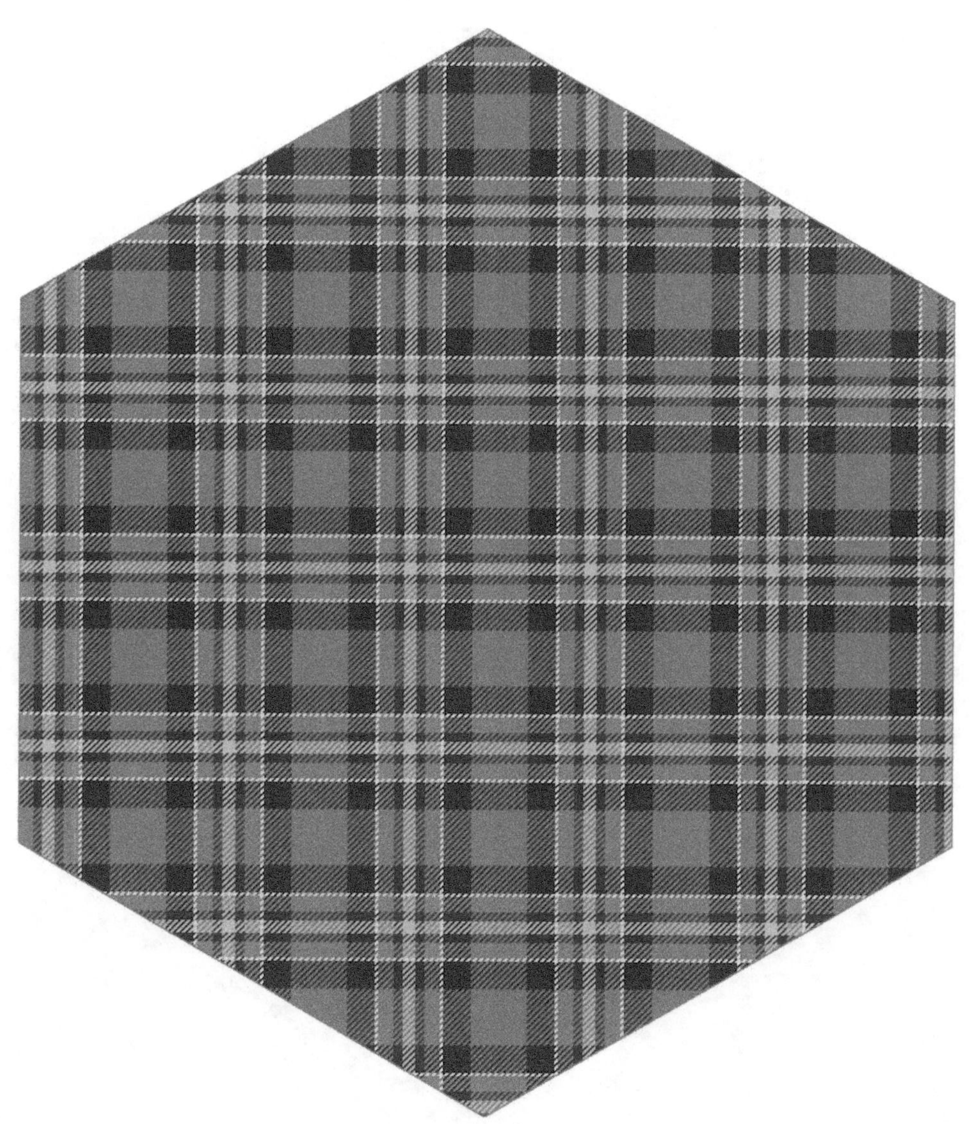

www.ingramcontent.com/pod-product-compliance
Lightning Source LLC
LaVergne TN
LVHW010621100826
845148LV00014B/3067

* 9 7 9 8 2 1 8 6 9 7 0 4 4 *